Forty

THE AGE AND THE SYMBOL

Forty

THE AGE
AND THE SYMBOL

Stanley Brandes

THE UNIVERSITY
OF TENNESSEE PRESS
KNOXVILLE

*The paper in this book meets the guidelines for per-
manence and durability of the Committee on Produc-
tion Guidelines for Book Longevity of the Council
on Library Resources. Binding materials have been
chosen for durability.*

Library of Congress Cataloging in Publication Data

Brandes, Stanley H.
    Forty : the age and the symbol.
    Bibliography: p.
    Includes index.
    1. Middle age—Psychological aspects. 2. Forty (The
number)—Psychological aspects. 3. Aging—Psychological
aspects. 4. Critical periods (Biology) I. Title.
BF724.6.B73 1985   155.6   84-29920
ISBN 0-87049-463-5

TO MY PARENTS,
EMANUEL AND ANNETTE BRANDES

CONTENTS

ACKNOWLEDGMENTS

I decided to write a book about turning forty after delivering lectures on the topic to undergraduates at the University of California, Berkeley. To these students, as well as to my graduate assistants, I owe a debt of gratitude; it was their collective response to my classroom presentations that stimulated me to publish my data and interpretations. Among my students, Uli Linke and Marcelo Suarez-Orozco were particularly influential and helpful. In addition, a number of friends and colleagues — Stanley Chojnacki, Galit Hasan-Rokem, David Mandelbaum, Jesús de Miguel, John Ogbu, Joan Prat, and Tim White — suggested relevant bibliography that I might never have encountered on my own. I received useful editorial advice from Joel Altman, Grace Buzaljko, Judith Brandes, and William McKinley Runyan. I wish to thank all these people for their generous assistance.

In preparing this volume, I received encouragement and moral support from Richard Brandes, Alan Dundes, and William Simmons. Howard Gardner, in addition to making valuable comments on the manuscript, deserves special thanks for standing behind me devotedly from beginning to end. Without the unwavering optimism of all these people, this project might never have reached conclusion.

A sabbatical leave in the spring of 1983 offered me much-needed research time in which I could develop my ideas about adult development. Barbara Quigley typed the final manuscript in her usual expert fashion. In the Department of Anthropology at Berkeley, we all recognize our good fortune in having her secretarial services at our disposal.

Portions of this book were delivered as lectures at Hobart and William Smith Colleges; the University of California, Berkeley; and, in Israel, at Ben-Gurion University, Bar-Ilan University, and the Hebrew University of Jerusalem. Audiences at all these institutions made me feel the project was worthwhile. Finally, I wish to thank Marjorie Fiske and Daniel Levinson for offering me a sympathetic ear during various stages in my thinking about this topic. To them and to others whom I may have forgotten momentarily, but who have helped and inspired me in manifold ways, I offer my heartfelt gratitude.

BERKELEY, CALIFORNIA
OCTOBER 1984

Thus we see that we should not underestimate the significance of number, since in many passages of sacred scripture numbers have meaning for the conscientious interpreter. Not without reason has it been said, to praise God: *Thou hast ordered all things in measure and number and weight.*

— St. Augustine, *The City of God,* Book II, Chapter 30

In the year 1302, just after his banishment from Florence, Dante Alighieri began composing *The Divine Comedy*. Having reached his late thirties, and beset by unforeseen circumstances, he opened his poem with one of the most profound and powerful statements of the human condition ever formulated: "*Nel mezzo del cammin di nostra vita / mi ritrovai per una selva oscura / che la diritta via era smarrita* (In the middle of the journey of our life / I found myself within a dark forest / where the straight way was lost)." Continues Dante, "Ah, how hard a thing it is to tell of / that savage and harsh and dense forest / the thought of which arouses my fear! / So bitter is it that death is hardly more so."

It is often difficult to translate the concepts of one place and era into another, but if we were asked to provide a contemporary American rendition of this opening stanza, we might say that Dante was describing a mid-life crisis. I say *a* mid-life crisis because, for all we know, *the* mid-life crisis as a named, shared, readily recognizable phenomenon did not exist in early Renaissance Italy. In fact, as reported and popularized in the February 14, 1983, issue of *Newsweek* (Begley 1983), anthropologists have begun to mount considerable evidence from non-Western peoples—everyone, as the article states, "from macaques to Malays"—to demonstrate that middle age does not produce the sorts of psychological stress that seem to be encountered regularly among twentieth-century Westerners. The mid-life crisis—or mid-life transition, as some scholars prefer to call it (e.g., Clausen 1972; Levinson et al. 1978; Lowenthal et al. 1975)—would appear to be specific to certain cultures at particular periods of time. Indeed, if we can judge from the abundance of academic and popular literature on the topic, circumstances in the contemporary United States have favored the widespread appearance of this often painful, if sometimes productive, life experience. And yet there is no doubt that people at other times and places, as *The Divine Comedy* illustrates, have also felt its effects.

Despite flourishing research on adult development, there are still many aspects of the mid-life crisis that remain obscure. One such unknown is why the crisis is so often attributed to forty-year-olds. Does some shared physiological change precipitate a crisis, or do cultural circumstances influence the way we feel and behave at forty? By answering this question, we might hope to determine the relative impact of human biology and culture on the life course. We might state whether nature or nurture takes priority in defining our progression through the long trajectory from birth to death. This volume is, in large measure, directed toward that overall problem.

THE GOALS OF THIS BOOK

In this study I intend to explore a single aspect of the mid-life crisis: the widely recognized importance of the age forty.

Among academic and popular psychologists in the United States, it has become common to cite age forty as a turning point, the time when we leave one stage of life behind and enter another. To these writers—virtually unchallenged experts in the field of adult development—the age of forty represents an unstable moment, flanked before and after by periods of relative equilibrium. But belief in the significance of forty as a watershed is hardly limited to the scientific world. It in fact constitutes one of our most tenaciously held and widespread folk notions about the life course.

Although all life transitions are by definition unsettling, the age forty seems to have earned a particularly notorious reputation. It is regularly portrayed as a time of emotional upheaval, when individuals lose the firm control over their lives that they had developed throughout the course of several preceding decades. Forty-year-olds, it is said, suffer an identity crisis. Men are reported to abandon their jobs, leave their wives and children; housewives to spruce themselves up, acquire lovers, and enter the job market. Such events, we are told, may be temporarily harmful, but as they are described in the literature, they usher in a new life stage in which the individual acquires deeper insight and a more highly integrated personality structure than before.

These notions, as I intend to show, are integral to the way most Americans think about the life course. Indeed, the age forty is so commonly pictured as transitional—in newspapers, magazines, and daily conversation—that people simply assume the occurrence of an emotional crisis at this time. The "forty-year-old jitters," as anthropologist Jules Henry once called the syndrome (1973, 128–48), are popularly reputed to be a natural, regularly expectable feature of life.

My own anthropological training has led me to suspect that any personality syndrome that is widespread and firmly believed in probably has a cultural rather than an organic órigin. In the 1920s, when Margaret Mead carried out her Samoan research, she was similarly skeptical with regard to an issue that bears very much on the one addressed in this volume. As is well known, Mead went to Samoa to demonstrate the relative insignificance of biological factors in the formation of adolescent personality. She believed that if teenaged Samoans could be shown to avoid the emotional turmoil characteristic of their American counterparts, then we could assume that cultural, rather than physiological, processes account for adolescent unhappiness in the United States. It was integral to her project, too, to discover whether adolescence was defined as a separate stage of life in Samoa, as it is in America. She found out, of course, that adolescence was not so defined; nor was it a period of expectable turbulence. She therefore concluded that the particular constellation of social and cultural circumstances prevailing in the United States must account for American adolescent unrest.

In the concluding chapter of this volume, I discuss the ongoing debate that Mead's research has occasioned, and its relation to my own findings about the age forty. After all, popular views regarding the age forty bear many similarities to those relating to adolescence. Both age periods are considered emotionally tumultuous; both, too, are said to be life turning points. My basic conclusion parallels Mead's: there are cultural, rather than biological, reasons why the age forty is perceived as transitional and why it is accorded such an unfavorable image. That many Americans undergo unhappy experiences at forty is undeniable. But the popular and scientific conception of forty-year-olds as almost genetically programmed to undergo a life transition is hardly defensible.

To formulate my opinions, I have relied on a wide array of sources: literature, folklore, religion, pop psychology, scholarly research, and personal observations. If at times I seem to judge folkloristic or literary evidence as on a par with scientific findings, it is because I believe that scholarship, objective though it may appear, is inevitably influenced to a greater or lesser degree by the cultural milieu in which it is produced. Hence, from the perspective of this essay, academic treatises are as much a product of culture as are proverbs or biblical injunctions. In fact, one of my major goals is to show that psychological scholarship, in particular, may be read as much for what it reveals about our cultural assumptions as for what it conveys about the subject under explicit investigation. Unwittingly, life-span psychologists (the usual denomination for scholars who specialize in adult development) have adopted culturally defined categories and boundaries. At least with regard to their view that forty represents a developmental turning point, they unconsciously reveal their cultural conditioning. I hope that by demonstrating this point, I underscore the need for a generally critical posture regarding ideas about transitional ages and stages.

PERSONAL INFLUENCES ON THIS RESEARCH

In my own discipline of anthropology, it has become pretty well established that no study can "be understood independently of the experience which produces it" (Berreman 1972, vii). Just as in the case of a traditional ethnography that is carried out via field techniques, the observations and information that underlie interpretations in a work like this are inseparable from the author's personal circumstances and intellectual biases (cf. Scheper-Hughes 1983). I therefore wish to mention a few of the most important recent influences on my thinking, including how I came to select the subject of adult development for investigation.

I have always believed that scholars choose their fields of study and research topics according to emotional as much as intellectual considerations. In the present case, I became interested in the age forty as I approached it. Several years prior to my fortieth birthday, at some indeterminate moment, I began for the first time in my life to feel uneasy about my age. Uppermost in my mind was that forty represented a turning point, fraught with unfulfilled ambitions and severely limited opportunities. To be sure, I could reflect on what others might consider substantial achievements in professional and family life, but somehow these paled beside the imminent arrival of a date—my fortieth birthday—when disturbances would inevitably occur.

If memory serves me, these feelings emerged independent of anything I had consciously sought to investigate, or even merely to read. Soon enough, however, they prompted me to peruse some of the many psychology volumes on midlife crises that can be encountered in almost any bookstore, and these studies began to reinforce my intuition that forty is indeed different from other ages. Other people—in the reports, mostly men but sometimes women as well—were going through the same emotional stage that I was experiencing. And yet when I spoke to friends about my experience, I encountered a mixture of opinions: for some, forty was significant; for others, the turning point came at thirty, fifty, or sixty.

No matter what the individual response, I came to be able to predict at least two types of reactions during the course of this study. First, there was virtually nobody for whom the age forty failed to evoke some special associations. Even if friends and colleagues had not themselves undergone a transition or crisis at this time, they would inevitably recount evidence that this age indeed marks a developmental watershed. Hence, anthropologist Nelson Graburn at the University of California, Berkeley, dismissed forty as holding any significance for him personally. Since he was born and bred in England, however, he was able to recall an oft-cited developmental sequence for men of the British elite: it is said that when such men reach forty, they begin to turn away from their wives and seek sexual services outside their marriage and class. Whether or not this actually occurs, nobody has ventured to prove. What is important from our point of view is that people claim that it happens. Child psychologist Howard Gardner, upon learning of my project, suggested that perhaps thirty-five — half the biblical life span — was at least as critical a turning point as forty. And yet he immediately recalled that whenever professional athletes turn forty, their continued active participation in the sports world becomes newsworthy. A third colleague, dismissing my observations as relevant to her own life, assented that forty must be meaningful, for at that age members of the exclusive Junior League undergo a major promotion in the organization's status hierarchy. In short, everybody seems to know somebody for whom forty is a developmental watershed.

The second predictable reaction to my project came mainly from people of about sixty years old and over. These individuals, principally women, tended to downplay the significance of forty. In conversation after conversation they would try to assure me that now that life expectancy has increased well into the seventies, forty represents no great transition. In their words, "They used to say that forty was important, but no longer." Whether these people, looking back at their mid-lives, minimized their actual feelings at the time they turned forty, or whether their opinion is an accurate description of their experiences, is impossible to determine at this time. However, I am certain of one thing: in the past twenty years, for reasons that are discussed fully in ensuing chapters, the significance of forty has changed. Whereas it used to signify the beginning of old age, the commencement of the last stage of life, it now symbolizes middle age and the beginning of middle adulthood. An individual of sixty-five or seventy naturally would have been socialized to the former meaning. It is understandable that forty should be dismissed by an older person who prefers to think of herself at the beginning of old age, rather than as having already been old for a period of twenty-five or thirty years. Rejecting forty as significant in this case is probably wishful thinking, designed to preserve a youthful self-image.

In my own case, especially as I write this essay in my fortieth year, I am all too aware that the age forty has acquired an importance in our own culture far beyond what might be expected by chance. In statistical terminology, forty is overdetermined. The net effect of this situation is that people who experience change at age forty can explain it away as a predictable occurrence; so can their friends and families. Merely recognizing this process, then examining the reasons behind it, has helped me to overcome my own trepidation about turning forty. I imagine that the same realization can similarly help others.

INTELLECTUAL INFLUENCES

In addition to personal experiences, there are a number of critical intellectual influences that have brought me to this study. Probably most outstanding is the comparative perspective that is the hallmark of anthropology and that has definitively shaped my thinking. Anthropologists are best known for studying exotic, nonliterate peoples; yet even the founders of our discipline, both in America and Europe, devoted themselves from time to time to examining their own society. In recent decades, this practice has become so common (due in part to intellectual considerations and in part to political and economic limitations on research abroad) that it is a regular and fully accepted feature of anthropological research.

What is perhaps distinctive about the anthropological view of one's own society, however, is that it derives its inspiration from implicit or explicit comparison with other groups. Sometimes the points of comparison come from reading and study; sometimes, as in my own case, they come from long-term field experiences in other cultures. When one immerses oneself in another culture, one tends to perceive one's own society through the eyes of one's informants.

I have had this experience many times. Since 1967, when I began carrying out fieldwork in rural Mexico, my family and I have lived for a total of some five years in four different Hispanic settings. This includes more than a year each among humble farmers and artisans in central Mexico, Old Castile (Brandes 1975), and Andalusia (Brandes 1980), plus a year in Barcelona. In each instance, I have constantly drawn comparisons among these groups as well as between them and my own middle-class American milieu. Never have I systematically analyzed the differences I perceive, but always they have helped me adapt to new settings and provided research clues.

In none of my field settings have I encountered the concern with the age forty that I myself have felt and that emerges in the popular and academic American literature on adult development. In fact, in Tzintzuntzan, the pottery-producing village in central Mexico where George Foster, Mary L. Foster, I, and several others have carried out extensive research, many—perhaps most—people do not even know their age. It has been a source of mild amusement that when some of our village friends and informants suddenly become interested in knowing how old they are, they ask us to consult our records (acquired from civil and baptismal registers) on their behalf! In fact, in all the rural settings where I have worked, there is considerably less age consciousness, and therefore less knowledge about people's ages, than typically exists throughout the United States. Perhaps the celebration of saints' days, rather than their own birthdays, which occurs among many Roman Catholic peoples, is part of the reason why age is less significant. My suspicion, however, and one that I will explore more fully in subsequent chapters, is that socioeconomic circumstances are what really count. This opinion would be borne out, for example, by the case of Barcelona, a sophisticated, urban, industrial city where age-consciousness most closely approximates that of American cities where I have lived. Still, not even the Catalan bourgeoisie of Barcelona focuses on the age forty to the extent that Americans do. These experiences abroad have aroused my curiosity about our own way of thinking and have caused me to ask, why forty?

Ironically, the very field experiences that provided a contrast to our own age-consciousness in the United States also led me to the partial answer. Given that Hispanic societies are basically Mediterranean in origin and contour, I became increasingly aware of the emphasis on the number forty throughout ancient Jewish, Christian, and Muslim civilizations, all of which were of course centered in the Mediterranean basin but have exerted an enormous influence on our own culture. After examining the evidence, I decided that the symbolism of the *age* forty is intimately tied to the symbolism of the *number* forty; the recognition of this symbolic equivalence, in fact, provides a good part of my argument, if not by any means the total explanation.

A second, related intellectual influence comes from the structuralist literature in anthropology that deals with numbers and their cultural consequences. I am reminded in particular here of Alan Dundes's well-known exploration of the number three in American life. Through an exhaustive examination of tripartite patterning in music, folklore, religion, syntax, and a host of other domains, Dundes concludes that "trichotomy exists but it is not part of the nature of nature. It is part of the nature of culture" (Dundes 1978b,

155). Likewise, in thinking about the age forty, I was inevitably drawn to the appearance of this number in religion and folklore, going all the way back—as I have said—to the ancient Middle East. In the Judeo-Christian tradition, forty —like three, twelve, seven, and ten—is a formulistic figure, imbued with special, sometimes sacred, significance. These numbers pervade our speech and thought and exert subtle influences on behavior. Without being able to prove the matter in any rigid scientific sense, I explore in subsequent chapters the possible impact of the formulaic forty on psychological theories as well as on human behavior.

I have also been affected by the highly innovative approach of anthropologist Misia Lipschutz Landau. In an unpublished doctoral dissertation from Yale University (1981), Dr. Landau examines paleoanthropological writing as a genre of literature; that is, she looks at influential nineteenth- and early twentieth-century writing about human evolution in the normally literary terms of plot, character, and theme. Taking her cues from folklorist Vladimir Propp (1958), she finds that early evolutionary writers told a story that had much in common with folktale and myth. It was a story based on a cultural model: that is, on an implicit system of elements and rules of which the authors themselves were unaware.

Similarly, without carrying the exercise too far, it may be fruitful to examine writing in developmental psychology from a literary standpoint. There are, to be sure, more than a few standard descriptions of the life course, each representing a sophisticated school of thought with its own eminent founders and intellectual traditions. Nonetheless, one of the most time-honored and widely shared human stories

14

is that which divides the period from birth to death into discrete segments, each with its own special characteristics and transitions. It is this developmental plot, and specifically the version that locates one of the critical turning points at age forty, that I explore in the following pages.

MY THESIS

In the end, this book reinforces a cultural perspective on the etiology of mental disturbance. The stance I shall take is the following: that the age forty is and has been important in Western civilization for centuries, but that it has assumed different symbolic meanings from one historical epoch to the next. In the present era, the age forty has played a prominent role in the increasingly evident definition of age grades. Popularization of this age as one in which critical personal transitions occur may actually have influenced the statistical frequency of mid-life crises, which in turn has reinforced popular impressions of the age forty as a period of vulnerability. Nothing biological produces emotional upheavals in forty-year-olds; rather, it is our culture, including our psychological theories, that imbues forty with special meaning and thereby exerts a subtle, unconscious influence on many of us.

An important facet of the proof for this position comes from the impact of changing sex roles on our ideas about life transitions. Specifically, women until recently have remained relatively immune to the mid-life crisis at forty. Their own developmental cycle has been perceived, rather, as being linked to such biological processes as the onset of menstruation and menopause. In recent years, however, women have become blanketed in with men, for whom forty has long been a turning point. We can see here, as in so many other domains of life, that women are increasingly defined with greater reference to culture, lesser consideration to nature. Equality does not always confer advantages. In this case, women now experience the traumas that were previously reserved for—or at least excused in—men.

Conceptions of the age forty and its role in the life course have profoundly influenced personal identity. In the United States, individual identities are produced by a complex interaction of ethnic, regional, sexual, occupational, and other considerations. We can state pretty confidently that one's generation is an important component of identity in virtually every known culture: to one degree or another, people everywhere measure and rank themselves relative to their ancestors and descendants, to their seniors and juniors. In only certain times and places, however, has absolute age—for example, reaching the age of sixteen or twenty-one or sixty-five—assumed major importance. We live in a society in which absolute ages such as these have acquired widespread symbolic meaning. It is to this type of age grading, and the role of forty within it, that we now turn.

When we think about the aspects of identity that currently engage the attention of Americans, adulthood and aging certainly rank among the most important. In a sense, the present era may be termed the age of adulthood, for it is one in which the consciousness of transformations that occur in the latter part of life has probably never been greater. This development is a logical offshoot of what Elizabeth Colson (1977, 190) has insightfully identified as the rapid appearance of "a full-blown age-grade system" in the United States. We have become more interested than ever in dividing the period between birth and death into discrete segments (Fry 1976, 176), and among these segments we are beginning to focus increasingly on middle and later life.

Whether or not clearly definable life stages, as such, actually exist—that is, whether people undergo regular, predictable transformations of life structure at certain ages— can be and has been debated (Riegel 1975, 123; Kertzer and Keith 1984, 19–61). Nonetheless, considering the importance of stages in the most influential schools of child development (e.g., Freudian, Eriksonian, Piagetian), it is hardly surprising that this perspective should have been adopted within the field of adulthood and aging, too. The prevalent view of adulthood today divides the life span into a series of more or less discrete stages. Within each stage, a state of relative equilibrium prevails, but there may exist unstable transition points or crises between stages.

It is in this context that forty plays a pivotal role. Age forty is one of the most commonly cited dividing points between stages of adult development. Traditionally, and until World War II, it was the time that people were considered to enter old age. Although this meaning persists somewhat into the present, the age forty increasingly has come to represent middle age. In fact, it is popularly thought to be the quintessential age at which men and women experience a mid-life crisis. In this chapter, we shall explore forty not only as a life turning point but also as a time of emotional, organic, and professional instability.

We deal here with well-entrenched stereotypes of the life course. Robert LeVine's concept of "life plan," as an "organized system of shared ideals about how life should be lived and shared expectancies about how lives are lived" (LeVine 1980, 82) fits my meaning. We are especially concerned with cultural expectations. Americans have certain beliefs about what constitutes a normal progression through the adult years. These beliefs explicitly or implicitly accord a large role to the age forty. It is these shared understandings about what happens at forty—whether articulated by scholars or laymen —that we now examine.

FORTY AS THE GREAT DIVIDE

Consider, first, forty as a demarcator of life stages, as a developmental boundary. Prior to World War II, writers seem to have taken this age to represent the dividing point between two major periods of life: youth and seniority. For instance, G. Stanley Hall, who was among the earliest life-span psychologists, was also one of the first scholars to seize on the age forty as a critical turning point. Having already completed his influential *Adolescence* in 1904 (a study that, in fact, helped to define this period as a distinct life stage), Hall went on to publish *Senescence: The Last Half of Life* (1922). When, in the introduction to this massive tome on aging, Hall compared his two research experiences, he decided that "youth is an exhilarating, age a depressing, theme. Both have their zest but they are as unlike as the mood of morning and evening, spring and autumn" (1922, viii). Hall's volume was explicitly devoted to describing people over forty, who, for him, had entered the period of "senescence." He firmly believed that "the phenomena of age begin in the early forties, when all should think of preparing for old age."

If old age was depressing for Hall, it was just the opposite for Walter B. Pitkin. Pitkin's 1932 best seller, *Life Begins at Forty*, apparently heartened a generation of Americans who—no doubt influenced directly or indirectly by Hall—apparently believed that once past forty, they were at death's door. Despite the fact that Pitkin had spent his own fortieth year in the midst of a world war and that at the time of his book's publication the country found itself in the worst economic depression in its history, Pitkin (1932, 3) seemed to express nothing but optimism about being older than forty:

> You who are crossing forty may not know it, but you are the luckiest generation ever. The advantages you are about to en-

joy will soon be recited with a sincere undertone of envy. The whole world has been remodeled for your greater glory. . . . Every day brings forth some new thing that adds to the joy of life after forty. Work becomes easy and brief. Play grows richer and longer. Leisure lengthens. Life's afternoon is brighter, warmer, fuller of song.

Although Pitkin did allow that "after forty, sensible people lead the Simplified Life" (p. 49), he generalized from his own experience in which, as he said, "life after forty has been much more exciting and profitable than before forty" (p. 11).

In his opinion that forty marks a critical turning point between two major life phases, Pitkin echoed not only the academic psychology of Hall but also the depth psychology of Carl Jung. In 1931, Jung had published a ground-breaking essay, "The Stages of Life," which explicitly defined forty as transitional: "Statistics show a rise in the frequency of mental depressions in men about forty," he claimed (1969, 395). Poetically metaphoric as ever, Jung compared the life course to the rising and setting of the sun, with age forty providing the "noon" of existence. Not only does an emotional transformation occur at this time, he said, but also "the reversal of the sun at noon changes even bodily characteristics. Especially among southern races one can observe that older women develop deep, rough voices, incipient moustaches, rather hard features and masculine traits. On the other hand the masculine physique is toned down by feminine features, such as adiposity and softer facial expressions" (1969, 397–98).

Although distinctive literary moods pervaded the works of the scholar Hall, the clinician Jung, and the popularizer

Pitkin, they all perceived forty as a critical divider between two major life periods. This idea is still very much with us. It appears, for example, in the choice of age cohorts for psychological analysis: Honzik and MacFarlane (1973), in a study of personality development and intellectual functioning, select a sample of subjects ranging in age from twenty-one months to forty years, thereby tacitly establishing age forty as the terminal point of a major life period. In the domain of popular psychology, forty is variously described as life's "mid-point" (Peterson 1967, 19), "half-way mark" (Purtell 1963, 11), and "point of the 'great divide'" (Harris 1975, 72), as well as a "frightening pivot point between the up and down of life" (Still 1977, 7). Sometimes contemporary book titles alone reinforce the same well-entrenched notion, as with *New Life Begins at Forty* (Peterson 1967) and *Life after Youth: Female, Forty—What Next?* (Jacobs 1979).

Throughout this century, then, forty has been taken as a significant turning point, cutting the life span neatly in two. To some observers this age signifies organic and professional decline; for others it represents the emergence of new opportunities. No matter what the interpretation placed on this age, however, it commonly provides a watershed between youth and seniority.

FORTY AS MARKING MIDDLE AGE

But age forty has not only been portrayed as slicing the life trajectory in two. Since World War II, it has also been increasingly incorporated into a relatively new conception of the life course, one that includes a discrete, clearly bounded middle age. In these recent studies, forty is used above all to define the beginning of the middle years. Alternatively, it might be cited as the single age that is most representative of the mid-life, or the age during which people are most likely to suffer from mid-life problems. For example, in *The Middle-Age Crisis* (1967), Barbara Fried repeatedly refers to middle-aged Americans as "Forties," with a capital F. For her, forty-year-olds are prototypical victims of the emotional traumas that appear in the middle years. Nancy Mayer expresses the same idea in *The Male Mid-Life Crisis: Fresh Starts after 40* (1978).

Among depth psychologists, Erik Erikson is probably the earliest and certainly the most influential thinker to express an association between age forty and middle age. At least some versions of his well-known series of eight psychosocial stages of development incorporate forty as a turning point. Specifically, at or around forty the sixth stage — that of generativity versus stagnation — becomes a developmental issue in the individual's life. By this age, occurring in the middle of the life span, people have worked out the basic outlines of their existence; they must now confront the question of whether to remain productive, creative, and active in the transmission of skills and knowledge to younger generations, or fall into a rut and cease to lead satisfying lives (Erikson 1963). Other scholars, like Linden and Courtney (1953) and Soddy and Kidson (1967), similarly associate both the definition of mid-life stages and the occurrence of mid-life crises with the age forty. Nowhere is this association more overt, however, than in Daniel Levinson's *Seasons of a Man's Life* (1978), in which forty is named as the approximate age when "Middle Adulthood" begins; forty, for this author and his colleagues, also marks the onset of a so-called "Mid-Life Transition."

To be fair, none of these life-span psychologists adheres rigidly to the notion that age forty inevitably harbors abrupt personality changes. Levinson, for example, believes that in some instances transitions occur gradually, even imperceptibly (Levinson et al. 1978, 198). And other scholars (e.g., Bühler 1968, 186; Jacques 1965, 502) cite different ages as pivotal. Nonetheless, there is no doubt that forty is the single most frequently named watershed. (See, for example, the excellent compilation of age categories as used by psychologists and reported in Fry 1976, 171.)

Even a subtle theorist like Orville Brim, who rejects outright any necessary correspondence between ages and stages, is able to write: "There is no evidence that [mid-life changes] are related to chronological age in any but the most general sense, e.g. 'sometimes during the forties'" (1976, 8). Brim's example, supposedly chosen arbitrarily, reveals the almost inevitable influence of the number forty on our thinking about adult development.

Hence, whether forty marks the beginning of old age or represents a middle stage of adulthood (e.g., Cain 1964; McGill 1980), it is perceived as a turning point. This perspective has been widely adopted in both popular and academic psychology.

SYMPTOMS AT FORTY:
DISSATISFACTION AND DEPRESSION

But why is forty popularly perceived as such a threshold? Why should reaching this age produce feelings of discomfort? The answer to this question is complex, but we can come to an initial understanding through an examination of presumed symptoms at forty. If we consider what people believe will happen to them at forty, or what they have reported about their concrete experiences at this age, then we can begin to comprehend their uneasiness.

We can identify at least three general types of transformation. The first can be described as a diffuse feeling of restlessness and unhappiness that overtakes the forty-year-old and possibly leads to family breakups. Barbara Fried (1967, 11–12) effectively summarizes the stereotype, at least as it applies to men:

> Forty is a noticeably restless, introspective, morose, moody, peevish, and melancholy person. . . . When asked to describe his life, Forty will reply vaguely that it is "awful," "boring," "dull," or "depressing," without being able to say exactly why. Thirty is satisfied with familiar surroundings and content to play with his own toys. Not so Forty, who instead is continually on the lookout for greener pastures and who spends much time day-dreaming about running away with someone who really appreciates him. Forty tends to be morbidly convinced that he is actually very sick (brain cancer and heart trouble are two especially favored diagnoses), and to grieve over the degeneration, both real and imagined, of his physical and mental capacities. It is not too much to say that Forty manages to make life miserable for those who must live with him, possibly because he seems unable to live with himself.

This mixture of rebelliousness, narcissism, hypochondria, and depression is the characteristic portrait of forty-year-olds that we encounter over and over.

This characterization appears in the mass media as well as in academic monographs. For example, a Peanuts cartoon sequence portrays a telling encounter between Charlie Brown and Lucy, here playing her familiar psychiatrist role. Charlie Brown confides that he's worried about his dad because "every night he sits in the kitchen eating cold cereal and looking at the pictures in his old high school year book." "How old is your father?" asks Lucy, to which Charlie Brown responds, "I think he just turned forty." "Nothing to worry about," advises Lucy. "He's right on schedule!" In the scientific domain, Daniel Levinson reports that for the vast majority of his varied occupational sample, age forty is "a time of moderate or severe crisis. Every aspect of [the informants'] lives comes into question, and they are horrified by much of what is revealed. They are full of recriminations against themselves and others. They cannot go on as before, but need time to choose a new path or modify the old one" (Levinson et al. 1978, 199). These images, like countless others, reflect the vague yet potent state of unhappiness that is supposed to be symptomatic of forty-year-olds.

SYMPTOMS AT FORTY: ORGANIC DECLINE

A second, more clearly definable symptom refers to the physiological aspect of aging: declining bodily strength, deteriorating appearance, reduced sexual energy, and related phenomena. Psychologists Joel and Lois Davitz express the predominant attitude perfectly when they state that "there seems to be no aging quite so devastating in this country as entering the forties" (1976, xv). Many Americans clearly believe that forty is when we cease being organically young.

This viewpoint can be traced at least as far back as the

Renaissance. Consider, for example, Shakespeare's second sonnet, probably the most eloquent lament of physiological transformations at forty ever written:

> When forty Winters shall besiege thy brow,
> And dig deep trenches in thy beauty's field,
> Thy youth's proud livery, so gaz'd on now,
> Will be a tatter'd weed of small worth held:
> Then being ask'd, where all thy beauty lies,
> Where all the treasure of thy lusty days;
> To say, within thine own deep-sunken eyes,
> Were an all-eating shame and thriftless praise.

Although one can always point to much about Shakespeare that is unique — above all, of course, his use of language — there is plenty of evidence that his work reflects the folk speech, wisdom, and theater of his day (see, e.g., Barber 1959; Dundes 1978a; Weismann 1978). It is probable, in fact, that he cites "forty Winters" as the time when the aging process becomes evident because that was the general opinion in early modern England: one of John Dryden's characters in *The Maiden Queen* (Act III, scene 1) states, "I am resolved to grow fat and look young till forty, and then slip out of the world with the first wrinkle and the reputation of five-and-twenty."

The age forty as a physiological turning point appears in later English literature, too. For example, this idea emerges in William Makepeace Thackeray's "Age of Wisdom" (1899):

> Ho, pretty page, with the dimpled chin
> That never has known the barber's shear,
> All you wish is women to win,
> This is the way that boys begin.
>   Wait till you come to Forty Year.

Also from the Victorian era comes the Harrow Football Song (Bennett, 1969), in which youthful singers look apprehensively toward the day when

> Forty years on, growing older and older
> Shorter in wind as in memory long
> Feeble of foot and rheumatic of shoulder
> What will it help you that once you were strong?

Forty has thus had a long symbolic association with physiological aging.

Once we become aware of this symbolism historically, evidence for its continued influence in our own times becomes repeatedly apparent. For example, in a promotional scheme for skin conditioners, the St. Ives Swiss Discovery Company distributed sweepstakes tickets in a mass California mailing. Among the optional questions on the entry form was one about age. Contestants could respond by checking the appropriate age category; significantly, the largest single category was allocated to people forty and older. It is safe to assume that advertisers at St. Ives Swiss Discovery either themselves believe that men and women over forty require special cleansers, or presume that those in this age range *think* they need unique body treatment.

We in the contemporary United States are hardly alone in such attitudes. The press recently reported that in Israel, where smoking-related illnesses are rampant, parliament just passed a law prohibiting three types of models from display in cigarette advertisements: show-business celebrities; people wearing sports clothes or uniforms; and individuals younger than forty. The implication, of course, is that once you pass forty, you are unlikely to win over customers through good looks (San Francisco *Chronicle,* 4 January 1983, p. 13). The image of the physiologically deteriorated forty-year-old is well entrenched in Western and related cultural traditions.

SYMPTOMS AT FORTY: CAREER CHANGES

The third specific symptom at forty is the occurrence of an occupational crisis. We are repeatedly reminded that suddenly, at age forty, people begin to reassess their careers and perhaps strike out in new directions. This is when they begin to feel trapped by jobs they no longer find satisfying, yet limited by the vast reduction of opportunity that confronts people of their generation. One of Henry Still's informants states the matter directly: "Folk wisdom says that you can do anything you want before 40 but after that you're locked. Coming up on 40 bothered me, physically and mentally" (1977, 201).

The popular media continuously reinforce our sense that the age forty represents an occupational turning point. For instance, an article about British mystery novelist P.D. James reports that although she knew from childhood that she wanted to be a writer, difficult economic circumstances prevented her from fulfilling her ambition. James explains that a departure from this path occurred "on my fortieth birthday. I realized that there was never going to be a convenient time, that another year had gone by, and still I was not a writer" (quoted in Garchick 1982, 11). After turning forty, she began getting up each morning two hours earlier than usual in order to allow time to write, and thus changed the course of her career.

This life experience would seem to confirm the idea that age forty really does bring occupational transitions, yet the media also indicate that forty is often *thought* to be an occupational turning point without actually being one. An example of this phenomenon comes from movie director Martin Scorsese (of *New York, New York* and *Raging Bull* fame), who says:

> At 40, you do start to think about things differently. I must say, I can understand why people eventually stop making pictures—because to make films in such an impassioned way, you really have to believe in it, you've really got to want to tell that story, and after a while, you may find out life itself is more important than the filmmaking process. Maybe the answer for what the hell we're doing here has to be in the process of living itself, rather than in the work. . . . Of course . . . you're talking to a person who's leaving this Sunday to look for new locations for the next picture. (quoted in Kakutani 1983, 26)

Although Scorsese apparently believes that age forty actually marks an occupational turning point, he ends his interview by stating that he himself intends, at forty, to continue making movies.

This article provides an instructive contrast to a second newspaper account, about Mick Jagger of the Rolling Stones:

> Thirty-nine is a rough age. . . . Consider Mick Jagger. There have been rumblings of late that, after 20 years as rock 'n' roll's most celebrated player, he has grown weary of the game. So weary, in fact, that when he arrived in town recently to finish work on a new Rolling Stones concert film, he agreed to an interview on only one condition: no talk about music. Only movies.
>
> Is Jagger looking for a change of career? Have mid-life blues

set in? Jagger scoffed at the notion, his well-lined face crinkling into the youthful grin of the perennial schoolboy. "I'm very interested in movies," he said, "but it's not going to break my heart if they don't become the biggest thing in my life."

He leaned forward and added confidentially, "I'm just a singer really. Do you know what I mean? People tend to forget that." He flashed a sharp, ironic smile, as though his confession had an unspoken punchline. If so, it remained private. Jagger seems to be facing 40 with equanimity. . . .

He wan't being coy; his acting ambitions seem part of a genuine desire to escape, not enhance, the Jagger persona. "I've been playing the same character for a long time," he said wearily. "I'd like to entertain people in a different way." (London 1982)

This report obviously conveys the newspaperman's unequivocal opinion that forty represents a significant boundary between youth and old age. Even his representation of Jagger's looks ("the well-lined face crinkling into the youthful grin") imbues the age with an ambivalent, betwixt-and-between quality. When we turn to Jagger's testimony, however, there is mention neither of age nor of life transition. Yet the information in the article confirms that Jagger is considering some sort of career change, since he claims to be tired of "playing the same character for a long time."

Martin Scorsese and Mick Jagger thus express different, but probably equally widespread, social postures. Scorsese believes that the age forty is transitional, yet he seems to be undergoing no professional change; Jagger, by contrast, is passing through a classic mid-life redefinition of self at age forty without necessarily recognizing this age as significant. It appears that forty sometimes brings career changes, and sometimes is simply associated symbolically with such changes.

CREATIVITY AT FORTY

The symbolic association between professional change and the age forty is hardly recent in the United States. As early as 1905, William Osler, retiring from the presidency of Johns Hopkins University, expressed the view that forty-year-olds are constitutionally different from younger people, and that they should alter their occupational activities accordingly. In a controversial farewell address, he advocated that a teacher divide his working life into three parts: "study until 25, investigation until 40, professional until 60, at which age I would have him retired." The justification for relegating pure teaching (which is what Osler meant by "professional") to the later years was his strong belief in "the comparative uselessness of men above forty years of age": "Take the sum of human achievement in action, in science, in art, in literature," he said, "subtract the work of the men above forty, and, while we should miss great treasures, even priceless treasures, we should practically be where we are to-day" (1905, 707–08).

Osler simply posited an impressionistic opinion, but his contemporaries marshalled statistics to demonstrate the contrary point of view. E.G. Dexter, for example, found that of 6,983 men listed in the 1900 edition of *Who's Who,* the median age was fifty-four; only one-sixth of the individuals were under forty. Counting the women in *Who's Who,* as well, the proportion of individuals under forty increased somewhat, a fact that researchers of the day attributed to the observation that "for women . . . recognition comes earlier, and attractiveness of person has a greater premium here than with her brother" (reported in Hall 1922, 6).

Despite the antiquated tone of the turn-of-the-century debate, the issue it addressed is still very much with us. In innumerable ways, the age forty continues to be cited as a turning point in creativity. Elliott Jaques has advanced this idea with reference to musicians and artists (1965, 502–03), and Roger Gould (1978, 311) cites it in connection with psychoanalytic discoveries. When, in the 1960s, New York's Whitney Museum of American Art mounted the exhibition "Forty Artists under Forty" (Goodrich and Bryant 1962), the organizers were obviously guided by the same age marker.

The actual age at which talent manifests itself is, of course, highly debatable. More and more, scholars are impressed by the enormous plasticity of human abilities over the life span (e.g., Riley 1979; Baltes and Willis 1979), In fact, one can easily cite well-known figures in the artistic and scientific worlds to support almost any allegation regarding the peak age of creativity. As Hammel (1983) has recently pointed out with reference to studies concerning the careers of chemists and mathematicians, so many different criteria are applied to the notion of creativity or productivity that researchers of this topic naturally arrive at vastly conflicting results. Indeed, the selective examination of career patterns in any given field might well indicate transitions of one kind or another at virtually every adult age.

It is forty, however, that seems to have attracted major attention as a professional turning point, at least in the popular mind. One of Nancy Mayer's informants articulated a good part of the reason why when he told her, "I suppose in society's terms turning forty is symbolic" (1978, 58).

Small wonder, then, that when Jack Benny refused to grow older than thirty-nine, all America laughed. Like most successful humorists, Benny had hit upon a sensitive issue in the personal lives of his public. By openly expressing his anxiety about reaching forty and the fantasy of never having to do so, his joke about aging became proverbial.

Even today, in the 1980s, there is reason to believe that Benny's joke still echoes popular sentiment. Just consider the following poem, composed by a grandfather for his grandchild and published recently by Ann Landers (Berkeley *Gazette*, 20 May 1983):

Advice to Adolescents

Enjoy your age before it's past.
Don't try to be 18 so fast.
You're only 14 once, my dears.
You'll be 39 for several years.

The joking reluctance to turn forty perhaps provides more evidence about the importance of this age to Americans than whatever knowledge we might gain through scientific tests and interviews. If nothing else, it confirms our view that forty is indeed a symbolic turning point. Let us now examine some ideas that have been advanced to explain how this symbolism developed.

XL CHAPTER THREE.
SOME POSSIBLE
EXPLANATIONS

We now turn our attention to the possible reasons why age forty has assumed such exaggerated significance. Why forty, rather than thirty-six or fifty-four? Why, when we consult the dozens of self-help manuals that are designed to lift the spirits of middle-aged men and women, do we discover that these books are directed toward people forty and over? A number of explanations, based on demographic, social, and economic circumstances, have been advanced to explain this phenomenon. Let us examine them in turn.

FORTY AS STATISTICAL MID-LIFE

The most obvious explanation for forty as a turning point is that it actually represents mid-life in a chronological, rather than a merely symbolic, sense. Certainly, as indicated in chapter 2, an abundance of popular and scientific writers foster this point of view, whether implicitly or explicitly. Their opinions, however, can be evaluated only with reference to a series of very different definitions of what constitutes the life span.

Life span, first of all, refers to the average length of life within any given group, whether that group be women, joggers, scientists, or the United States population as a whole. If we calculate along these lines, we can arrive at a mean value for whichever segment of the population happens to interest us. To arrive at an average mid-life of forty, in the statistical sense, there would have to exist an average life span of eighty. That is, if we could prove that people on the whole live to be about eighty, then we might justify using forty to indicate the midpoint of life.

Unfortunately, no evidence exists to confirm these statistical means. Not only has the average life span among Americans never been as high as eighty, but it also seems improbable that it has ever been that high at any other time or place. Logic itself argues against forty as a statistical midpoint. Average life spans vary within populations: as is well known, men and women, American blacks and whites, urbanites and rural people all form contrasting pairs with respect to life span. Even if it were possible to demonstrate that the mean life span for any of these groups is or has been eighty, we would still need to explain why forty should be cited as *the* single midpoint of existence universally.

A second possible interpretation of life span is the maximum age that one can reasonably hope to live. A familiar passage from biblical Psalm 90 tells us, "The years of our life are threescore and ten, or even by reason of strength fourscore." But this maxim has seldom been taken to indicate the actual state of affairs in any literal sense, either in ancient times or contemporaneously. The most we can say is that seventy or eighty is the approximate age that at least some segment of humanity may expect to live. Approximations such as this, however, are insufficient to explain a highly concrete midpoint like forty.

Nor, as demographers Acsádi and Nemeskéri have indicated (1970, 15), has there been any success in determining the potential length of human life, in the abstract. There exist well-known records of exceptionally long life spans — for example, of the number of people aged one hundred or older in various countries — but the fact that these long-lived individuals cluster in developing or remote regions, which often use poor census-collecting techniques, leads to the suspicion that the data are inaccurate (1970, 20). In any event, these cases, like those of individuals throughout history who are said to have lived unusually long lives (1970, 16–17), cannot possibly influence prevalent Western views about life expectancy. Even if they did exert such influence, the midpoint of the average life span would turn out to be significantly higher than forty.

However, since forty is so prevalently seen as the midpoint of life, it seems reasonable to ask how many years most forty-year-olds might expect to live. Life expectancy constitutes yet another possible definition of the life span. Summarizing the *Statistical Abstracts of the United States* from 1973 (as good a year as any, considering the dates of the publications and other evidence that we have been examining throughout this volume), Bernice and Morton Hunt (1975, 24) conclude that "a man of 40 can expect to reach 72, and a woman of 40 can expect to reach 78 — a man of 65 can look forward not to just another 7 years but another 13, while a woman of 65 can look forward not to 13 more years but to 17 more." None of these age expectations, however, yields a midpoint of forty.

Daniel Levinson, drawing on suggestions made more than a half-century earlier by biologist G.P. Bidder, believes that changing life expectancies can explain why we perceive forty as a turning point. Primitive man, he says, seldom lived beyond forty: "By that age the children were grown, the best years of productive labor ended, the contribution to the tribe fulfilled. By 40 a man was obsolete." Now that life expectancies far exceed forty, Levinson says, we are still somehow unable to take the improved circumstances for granted: "Our profound anxiety at passing 40 reflects the ancient experience of the species: we still fear that life ends at 40" (Levinson et al. 1978, 328, 330).

Levinson's hypothesis, although interesting and provocative, is difficult to defend. For one thing, it is hard to believe that many non-literate peoples, whose languages did not even permit them to count above three or four with exactitude, could be conscious of an average or expected life span. For another, Levinson's theory presupposes a kind of collective memory, based on the experience of the species and transmitted genetically to contemporary humanity. There is no evidence that such a Lamarckian process has ever occurred. Finally, while it is possible to arrive at good fossil-age estimates in the case of young individuals, this is definitely untrue "when it comes to distinguishing a 30-year-old individual from a 40-year-old individual" (Stewart 1962, 143). Hence, it is difficult to understand the basis on which Levinson confidently cites forty years as the age when most individuals in the past could be expected to die. The hypothesis remains unproven.

Actually, the best reason to dismiss forty as a chronological midpoint comes from historical demography. Life tables over the first half of the twentieth century demonstrate immense variation in the mean length of life, with a steady trend toward increased longevity (Dublin, Lotka, and Spiegelman 1949). Even so, there seems to have emerged no single age to compete with forty as representing the major mid-life turning point. Even the changing symbolic significance of forty, from representing old age to representing middle age, does nothing to detract from the fact that forty has for decades — even, as we shall see, for centuries — stood for the main developmental watershed in adult life.

FORTY IN THE FAMILY CYCLE

A second possible explanation for the importance of forty is that this age coincides with critical changes in the developmental cycle of the family and/or household. A prominent school of life-span psychologists believes that the stages of development are defined by actual or anticipated changes in family and household structure, combined with career patterns. Tamara Hareven (1978a, 5) has provided an accurate summary of this analytical approach. It encompasses, she says, "individual development as well as the collective development of the entire family. It focuses on the meshing of individual careers with the family as it changes over time." Hence, when Marjorie Fiske Lowenthal and her associates (1975) examined life transitions in the San Francisco Bay area, they selected four sample groups: high school seniors, newlyweds, parents facing the postparental or "empty nest" stage of life, and people on the verge of retirement. In virtually all studies of individuals facing specific family circumstances, such as widowhood (e.g., Lopata 1975; 1980), we can assume that a similar perspective has been adopted. What emerges is a stage-like portrait of development, but with no consideration given to concrete ages.

Although theorists of this persuasion often reject the notion that adult development is determined by age, there are at least two ways in which forty might be seen to coincide with the family cycle and thereby indirectly acquire an importance of its own. First, the so-called empty-nest syndrome, as others have noted (e.g., Glick and Parke 1965; Rogers 1982, 197), often produces a temporary depression due to a perceived loss of life purpose; indeed, it is sometimes claimed that the mere anticipation of a childless home is sufficient to produce this sensation. Despite the undeniable prevalence of this kind of mid-life depressive episode and its probable coincidence with the approximate age forty for at least some people (especially those in which *anticipation* of the empty nest precipitates the crisis), there is no evidence that parents generally turn forty either when their last child actually leaves home or when this event is imminent.

In fact, considering that the empty-nest phase has altered considerably in duration over the past century (Glick and Parke 1965), while the age forty continues to be a conceptual life-span turning point, it would be difficult to claim the validity of this explanation. As Uhlenberg (1978, 89) has pointed out, it is practically impossible even to make an accurate estimate of the number of people who pass through this phase: "Women who die early, never marry, bear no children, or have their marriage disrupted early, never enter an empty-nest phase. Because of substantial variability in age at which the last child leaves home, it is difficult to estimate how many women experience this aspect of the life course." It is highly improbable that the empty-nest syndrome has exerted any causal influence on the importance of age forty.

A second aspect of the family cycle that might possibly produce the evident concern with the age forty is the coincidence between adolescence and what has been termed "midolescence" (McMorrow 1974); that is, as observers have already pointed out (e.g., Fried 1967, 59), many parents reach middle adulthood just about the time their children become adolescents. This circumstance is believed to promote a mutual reinforcement in the attitudes and behavior of the two generations; stated crudely, the society tacitly expects both age groups to go slightly crazy. As if on cue, the adolescent children and midolescent parents comply with this expectation. The children imitate their parents and viceversa.

Although this interaction undoubtedly occurs, at least in some families, it nonetheless cannot be marshalled as an explanation for the emphasis on forty. For one thing, people without children, as well as those with fully grown or very young children, also undergo what might be termed a mid-life crisis around the age of forty. For another, both the adolescent and midolescent years encompass a time span long enough that the focus on the specific age forty still remains a mystery.

PHYSIOLOGICAL AGING AT FORTY

If the family cycle cannot explain the emphasis on forty, is the aging process with all its physiological ramifications sufficient to do so? That is, do we have evidence that the symbolic association between age forty and organic deterioration, as examined in the preceding chapter, has a basis in reality?

Some researchers have, in fact, observed " a sense of bodily decline . . . a sense of aging—the feeling of being old rather than young" (Targ 1979, 377) in middle adulthood generally, and at age forty in particular. Forty is said to be significant for both sexes. Of men, Mayer has written (1978, 111–12) that "once a man is past forty his erection will take longer to achieve—minutes perhaps, as compared to seconds in his youth. It may not be as full or firm as when he was younger, and at the end of intercourse his penis will return to a relaxed state much more quickly than it used to." According to the same author, women take the opposite path: "Women are scarred most severely in their youth, when they are more strongly prohibited than men from obtaining sexual satisfaction. Their apparent sexual flowering around forty merely reflects a long process of shaking off old inhibitions."

Sociologist Ruth Harriet Jacobs (1979, 104) also reports that forty is physiologically significant for women. By this age, she claims, the initial panic that women experience with recognizing their first wrinkle or gray hair "hardens into a chronic condition." No wonder, with all the concern about the physical consequences of turning forty, that former pro football star George Blanda (1978) could publish a successful health manual directed toward an evidently vulnerable, captive audience; appropriately, the book is entitled *Over Forty: Feeling Great and Looking Good!*

Actually, the opinions of these writers are just that—

mere reflections of folk ideology rather than the result of scientific thought. There is, in fact, no good evidence that reaching the age forty in and of itself produces any dramatic alterations in physical and intellectual powers, except perhaps in individuals who might be influenced by the belief that this age *should* mark some dramatic physiological turning point. Consider, for example, recent studies of the relationship between aging and cognition, a mental process that is intimately bound to brain physiology. In a summary of research results, Howard Gardner (1982, 581) states:

> The picture one obtains of cognitive power in aging individuals depends on a variety of factors, with some research documenting declines . . . other investigations suggesting a steady course, particularly in individuals who remain healthy and active. . . . Some authorities have in fact tried to identify tasks at which older individuals actually excel. For instance, mature adults may be better able than adolescents to identify new problems in a domain of knowledge (such as science), rather than merely to solve problems posed by others. . . . The heights of creative invention, and the ability to forge powerful intellectual syntheses, often are not realized until mid-life.

Evidence is therefore uncertain and contradictory. There is as yet nothing of scientific merit to substantiate the claim that cognitive powers experience some cataclysmic decline at or around age forty.

Nor, contrary to popular opinion, can we say that there is a dramatic diminishing of sexual energy at this time. As far as endocrine changes are concerned, "from about thirty on there is a gradual decline in testosterone and cortisol and from thirty through the remainder of life there is a gradual decline in secretion of androgens for the male" (Brim

1976, 4). Without doubt, male sexual drive decreases with age, but this process generally occurs gradually and, except in cases of organic illness, would be difficult to link to any particular age, much less the specific age forty (Rogers 1982, 145–46). Of course, we must not discount the possibility of psychosomatic reactions. If men are told often enough that their sexual energies should decline at forty, then on reaching this age they may begin for the first time to notice the impact of long-term, gradual libidinal changes (Lear 1973, 61). Alternatively, other forty-year-old men, in tacit compliance with or defiance of life-course expectations, may actually reduce or step up their sexual activity. But these reactions are all independent of what we now know about normal male physiology.

As for women, the great physiological event of their middle years, of course, or at least the one that is commented upon most frequently in the literature, is menopause. In the contemporary United States there is a range of ages at which women experience the permanent cessation of ovulation. On the average, however, menopause comes to them at age forty-seven (Rogers 1982, 144), and there is mounting evidence that menopause produces no necessary negative psychological state (e.g., Brown 1982, 146–47). On the contrary, in an exhaustive study of middle-aged women in five Israeli subcultures (including Central Europeans, Turks, Persians, North Africans, and Arabs), it was discovered that menopause was heartily welcomed by all the women in the study sample: "Even those women who looked back with longing for children they had not borne when they were younger did not want to mother infants, or even to retain the potential for pregnancy" (Datan, Antonovsky, and Maoz 1981, 2). Menopause brought psychological relief rather than anxiety.

On several counts, then, we can dismiss the idea that women either experience a radical physiological shift at age forty or undergo anything like a mid-life crisis at that time. Both men and women, it seems, have been influenced by popular beliefs about age-linked physiological changes and their psychological consequences. Such changes, according to scientific evidence, neither generally nor necessarily occur at or around age forty and are therefore inadequate to explain the widespread attention given to this age.

PROFESSIONAL LIFE AT FORTY

As a final possible explanation for the age forty as a transition point, we may consider evidence that this age represents a cessation of employment opportunities, a severe limitation on career alternatives, and that these reduced life chances produce malaise, depression, or other forms of self-destruction. In the preceding chapter, we examined a number of testimonials to the fact that people often feel occupationally trapped at forty. To what degree does the age forty actually limit people's chances in the field of work?

There is no doubt that at least in Western industrial society, including our own, men and women over forty have long suffered from discriminatory employment practices. As early as the 1920s, W.R. Miles, an early life-span psychologist, was concerned about reports that workers over forty were having difficulty obtaining jobs in California; in response, he helped found the first major research unit devoted to

44

the psychological aspects of aging, at Stanford University in 1928 (Charles 1970, 44). Two decades later, resentment against age discrimination reached fever pitch with the publication of Conrad Miller Gilbert's *We Over Forty: America's Human Scrap Pile.* The author's anger can be gauged from his statement of the book's goals:

> *"Now is the Time to Fight"* can well become the slogan of men and women over forty who have been seeking an opportunity to secure gainful employment, and who have usually gotten the curt reply, "You are too old." . . . There are millions, yes, millions of men and women past forty who are seeking employment and who are barred on account of their age. These folks are the tragic figures of this era. . . . The purpose of this book is to arouse the interest of every man and woman over forty so that they will join with their fellows in a nation-wide movement to aid in the fight to earn an honest living. (Gilbert 1948, 12–13)

Gilbert predicted that about ten years after his book's publication, some drastic legislative changes would be made to avoid *"our present cruel and fantastic system of throwing able men and women on the human scrap pile just because they have reached an age when someone declares that they are too old to earn a living"* (1948, 5; original emphasis).

It seems that Gilbert's prediction was overly optimistic. The country had to wait until 1967 for Congress to pass the Age Discrimination in Employment Act (ADEA). The results of congressional inquiry into age prejudice are embodied within the ADEA itself. If only to confirm that such prejudice was not imaginary on Gilbert's part, it is worth quoting the document's preamble:

> The Congress hereby finds and declares that—
> (1) in the face of rising productivity and affluence, older

workers find themselves disadvantaged in their efforts to retain employment, and especially to regain employment when displaced from jobs;

(2) the setting of arbitrary age limits regardless of potential for job performance has become a common practice, and certain otherwise desirable practices may work to the disadvantage of older persons;

(3) the incidence of unemployment, especially long-term unemployment with resultant deterioration of skill, morale, and employer acceptability is, relative to the younger ages, high among older workers; their numbers are great and growing; and their employment problems are grave;

(4) the existence in industries affecting commerce, of arbitrary discrimination in employment because of age, burdens commerce and the free flow of goods in commerce. (Judges of the Federal Court 1976, 229)

With these circumstances in mind, Congress stipulated that the ADEA should cover cases of suspected discrimination against people specifically between the ages of forty and sixty-five. A 1979 modification of the ADEA raised the upper limit to seventy, but the lower figure — forty years of age — has remained constant (Federal Regulation of Employment Service 1981, 5).

In response to this legislation, there has been a spate of lawsuits (discussed more fully in the final chapter) against potential employers by forty-year-olds who believe that they have been the victims of age discrimination. For example, one male physicist has filed an age discrimination charge against the University of California. His suit claims that officials at UC campuses in Berkeley and Davis engaged in a "discrimination policy of hiring based on their belief that younger applicants are preferable to older applicants." The plaintiff states that UC officials told him on a number of oc-

casions "that they could hire younger people for less money."
He apparently based his claim specifically on age considerations: he was not hired, states his suit, because "he is over
40 years of age and . . . this discriminatory treatment has
been applied systematically and continually since 1966, just
after he attained the age of 40" (Berkeley *Gazette,* 11 Nov.
1982, p. 5).

Even in the academic world, then, where opportunities
and achievement are sometimes thought to expand indefinitely, doors begin to close at forty. Just consider the application guidelines for fellowships in Latin American studies
as offered by the Doherty Foundation. The foundation's criteria read: "Since one purpose of the grants is to increase
the number of young United States citizens who have had
field experience in Latin America, applications from persons over forty . . . will be considered only in exceptional
cases." In my own field of anthropology, too, the prestigious
Margaret Mead Award is restricted to scholars under forty.

Along the same lines, a survey from England indicates
that fully half the managerial and administrative positions
advertised in the British press stipulate an upper age limit
of forty (Still 1977, 134). Although, under the ADEA, age
discrimination in the United States may be less overt, there
is evidence that American men and women over forty still
feel an occupational crunch of one sort of another. For many
people, the pressure comes simply from remaining occupationally stationary and ceasing to experience the economic
and social mobility that characterized their earlier career
phases. Michael Richards, program director for the American Management Association, has stated that "only five out
of every 100 guys are going to get to the top jobs. The rest

47

are headed for trouble when they reach 40 to 50" (quoted in Still 1977, 131). Confirmation of this phenomenon comes from Nancy Mayer (1978, 54), who, after examining the relevant statistics, declares that "only a handful of highly educated men will continue to move up the ladder after forty, while the majority will merely hold onto whatever rung they have already reached. And some, usually the least educated, will start to slip down. . . . What this means for most men is no more pay increases or promotions after forty."

The connection between economic fate and the age forty is not only a modern phenomenon, however; evidence of its existence can be traced back at least as far as early modern Europe. In 1640, in *Jacula Prudentum,* George Herbert wrote, "He that is not handsome at twenty, nor strong at thirty, nor rich at forty, nor wise at fifty, will never be handsome, strong, rich, or wise." According to this view of the world, one achieves one's financial limit at forty. Edward Young declared in "Night Thoughts," about a century later: "At thirty, man suspects himself a fool / Knows it at forty, and reforms his plan." When applied to the realm of work, this poem expresses perfectly the feelings that have been described by many mid-career men and women in the twentieth century.

Of course, there is evidence, both historical and contemporaneous, that being over forty confers some occupational advantages as well. Particularly in the area of administration, some observers believe that older people, because of accumulated knowledge and experience, can make balanced judgments in a way that adolescents and young adults cannot (Flavell 1977; LaBouvie-Vief 1980). Howard Gardner remarks (1982, 581) that although these claims "have not yet

48

been confirmed in experimental investigations . . . the numerous societies . . . that confer the greatest responsibilities on individuals of middle and old age seem implicitly to confirm this positive view of their cognitive capacities." Recognition of this quality would seem to be embodied in requirements for holding political office. Historically, it has been common to restrict the highest, most difficult posts to people forty years and older, as discussed more fully in the following chapter.

Whether being forty confers or restricts occupational opportunities, there is no doubt that this age has been associated through the years, and certainly in present-day America, with career developments. Can we therefore assume that the importance of forty to finance and employment has actually created the current image of this age as being unstable and transitional?

I suggest that the causal chain is the reverse: that is, that the age forty has for centuries been perceived as transitional and that this perception has actually influenced career patterns and job opportunities. To understand why, we must now turn to a consideration of the number forty and its symbolic dimensions.

XL

In 1911, after celebrating his fortieth birthday, Theodore Dreiser embarked on a European journey. Three years later, *A Traveler at Forty,* the chronicle of his experiences, was published in New York. "When one turns forty and faces one's first transatlantic voyage, it is a more portentous event than when it comes at twenty," Dreiser explained (1914, 6). Exactly forty years after the publication of that book, a lesser-known author named Emily Kimbrough came out with *Forty Plus and Fancy Free* (1954) the story of her frolicking trip with four friends—all over the age of forty—to Italy, France, and England. Both travel accounts obviously attributed symbolic significance to the age forty; in some way or another, reaching this age provided their authors a release from past restrictions, offered them a new beginning. To Americans going abroad in the 1910s and even in the 1950s, the journey was sufficiently different from ordinary experience that it could in effect become the medium through which a new self was discovered and the old self left behind, whether temporarily or permanently.

Carl Jung, who was intensely interested in the symbolic significance of journeys (see, e.g., Jung 1961), would probably have appreciated these volumes for their implicit confirmation of his own ideas. For Jung and his followers (e.g., Maduro 1976), journeys are metaphors for inward transformations, or for new adaptations to the changing circumstances in which individuals find themselves. When people travel, according to the Jungian point of view, the journey is above all psychological or spiritual, and it is this aspect of Dreiser's or Kimbrough's experience that Jung would have ferreted from their accounts. Especially because Jung believed that the years after forty represent the "afternoon of life" and that "we cannot live the afternoon of life according to the programme of life's morning" (1969, 399), he would have doubtless perceived some sort of symbolic transformation in travel at age forty.

Actually, in dealing with the age forty, we encounter at least four distinct yet interrelated symbolic meanings, which have already emerged implicitly in the preceding chapters. Two of these relate to quantitative aspects of forty: as representing a great number in general, on the one hand; as standing for a specific number, on the other. The remaining two refer to more qualitative dimensions of the age forty: its representation of novelty, a new beginning, or rebirth; and its transitional overtones. But why should the age forty be imbued with such heavy symbolic import? What is it about this age that causes people to attribute to it a significance far out of proportion to what might be expected on the basis of statistical probability?

Having utilized the preceding chapter to discuss and then dismiss some possible explanations, I intend to devote the remainder of the book to analyzing what I believe can account for this phenomenon.

THE NUMBER FORTY

To begin, we must understand that the significance of the *age* forty derives in large part from the significance of the *number* forty. In the United States, we share with the rest of the Western world an implicit emphasis on certain numerical figures—including, among others, three, seven, ten, twelve, and forty—that have become formulistic. That is, we organize our lives with reference to these numbers and think of the world in terms of them with only the barest awareness, if any, that this is the case.

As pointed out in chapter 1, Alan Dundes (1978b) has convincingly demonstrated the covert influence of the number three on contemporary American life. In a creative piece of scholarship, he shows the relevance to our own lives of a mathematical figure that earlier writers had already established as culturally significant in different domains (e.g., Abbot 1962; Ben Cheneb 1926; Brough 1959; Deonna 1954; Dumézil 1958; Erben 1857; Glenn 1965; Goudy 1910; Gunther 1912; Heizer 1962; La Sorsa 1963; Lease 1919; Lehmann 1914; Paine 1901; Strand 1958; Tavenner 1916; Usener 1903). Similarly, other scholars have devoted themselves to the numbers four (e.g., Buckland 1895; Parsons 1916) and five (e.g., Geil 1926; Lowie 1925), which prove to be more consequential than three in various non-Western cultures.

Although even the most casual encounters with Western art and literature are bound to uncover at least a few references to the number forty, nearly three-quarters of a century has passed since there have been any scholarly studies devoted to this figure. The most thorough and far-reaching is *Die Zahl 40 im Glauben, Brauch und Schrifttum der*

Semiten (The Number 40 in the Beliefs, Customs and Scriptures of the Semites), a vast compendium published in 1909 by Wilhelm Heinrich Roscher (who later wrote a similarly extensive and carefully researched treatise on the number fifty [Roscher 1917]). Shortly thereafter followed a brief piece, "The Forty," by F.W. Hasluck (1912–13), who was unaware of Roscher's groundbreaking study at the time and who, in any case, focused on material from Turkey. More recently, Gabriella Eichinger Ferro-Luzzi (1974, 143–52) has provided an interesting discussion of numerology in India, where forty — among other numbers — bears symbolic salience for the populace at large, but especially for Muslims. These studies all suggest that forty has assumed special meaning for the peoples of the eastern Mediterranean. It is, in fact, highly likely that the importance we attribute to this figure derives ultimately from the ancient Mediterranean world. It is also probable that religious practices and linguistic conventions deriving from that region and era have exerted a subtle and covert, yet powerful, influence on our modes of speech and thought.

Evidence from ancient times to the present reveals at least four symbolic dimensions to the word and number forty. Heuristically, it is useful to distinguish these from one another, because they correspond to distinctive meanings that popular and academic psychologists attribute to the age forty. However, many data that I have classified under one symbolic dimension could easily be marshalled to illustrate the others. This polysemic quality of the number forty, as Victor Turner (1969) would call it, is probably one reason why forty has become formulistic, and why its linguistic and classificatory influence has expanded throughout the centuries. Along with three, seven, and a few other figures, it is among the most symbolically vigorous numerals in our vocabulary.

FACET 1: FORTY AS SYMBOLIZING MANY

First, there is forty as meaning many, a lot. After the specific reference of forty to the quantity forty, this symbolic meaning is the most common in our language, according to the Oxford English Dictionary (Murray 1933). Consider definition (b): "Used indefinitely to express a large number." This denotation has produced an abundance of colloquial expressions, some outmoded but others still in use (Partridge 1961a; 1961b). For example, a deceitful person can be called forty-faced, as in "forty-faced liar" or "forty-faced flirt." Clearly the implication here is not that the individual literally assumes forty different character roles, but rather that he or she tries to be many things to many people. An angry or alarmed person is said to "have forty fits," just as in some English dialects extreme distaste or utter contempt may be indicated by stating, "I wouldn't touch it with a forty-foot pole" (a variant of the ten-foot pole common in other dialects).

Throughout several centuries, until the beginning of the twentieth century, there were many similar expressions that are now either rare or extinct (Partridge 1961a; 1961b). In some regions a fat, dumpy person was called pejoratively a "forty-foot, forty-guts," referring to the square shape and large size of the individual. An excessive talker might be called "forty-jawed" or "forty-lunged," while a centipede (a name indicating one hundred feet) used to be termed a "forty-legs."

Among some British workers in the late nineteenth century, it was common to say in contempt or derision, "I wouldn't be caught dead in a forty-acre field with him (her)." A variant was "I wouldn't be seen crossing a forty-acre field with him (her)." To explain these colloquialisms, Eric Partridge, the late, great compiler of extra-official English, states: "To a Cockney 40 acres are a considerable area; *forty* is generic for a largish number" (Partridge 1961b, 1127). Of course, forty can also be a shorthand way of indicating a small quantity; since the mid-1820s the expression "forty winks" has been used to refer to a nap, a short sleep. But its meaning as "many" or "a lot" is and has been much more usual.

A closely related meaning, also recognized in the OED, is "with immense force or vigour," or "like anything." Hence, "forty to the dozen" used to mean very quickly; the sentence "He walked off forty to the dozen" meant "He left abruptly and rapidly." From about the turn of the present century, the expression "with forty pounds of steam behind him" meant more or less the same thing; a person receiving military orders, for example, could be described as responding in that fashion: that is, without delay. Inanimate objects, too,—such as streams or locomotives—could "go like forty," or run rapidly; this usage, at least in the United States, has been shown to exist as late as the 1940s (Mathews 1951, 649).

Forty was also used to express intensity, especially in mid-nineteenth-century America. Craigie and Hulbert (1940, 1047) report sentences from the period such as, "The teamsters boast a powerful horse that will pull like forty" or "[The officers were] all going it like forty at twenty-deck poker." Sam, a character in *Uncle Tom's Cabin* (Stowe 1852,

65), announces, "I has principles, and sticks to them like forty."

The sense of forty as indicating strength in numbers, speed, or feelings appears in a number of other extinct expressions as well. In the eighteenth and nineteenth centuries, "to weigh forty" meant to be worth a lot, to be expensive or valuable (Partridge 1949). Forty-rod was the designation for strong whiskey and rum in nineteenth-century America (Craigie and Hulbert 1940, 1047). Forty has also been employed to indicate relative, as well as absolute, strength: in 1873, Joaquín Miller, author of *Life amongst Modocs,* commented that "[The Indian children] were forty-fold more civil than are the children of the whites" (quoted in Craigie and Hulbert, 1047). Such explicit comparative usage can be traced at least as far back as Shakespeare; speaking of Ophelia (Act V, scene 1), Hamlet asserts: "Forty thousand brothers / Could not, with all their quantity of love / Make up my sum." In *The Merry Wives of Windsor,* we read, "I had rather than forty shillings I had my Book of Songs and Sonnets here" (Act I, scene 1).

The quotation from *Hamlet* indicates that forty is sometimes combined with thousand to yield the effect of great quantity or strength. It may be that forty as symbolizing the general quality of strength comes to English through phonological assimilation with the French *forte,* although the evidence from the Middle East would suggest otherwise. The Bible, for example, commonly refers to "forty thousand" when describing large numbers. Hence, in the Old Testament we read that forty thousand people prepared for the battle of Jericho (Joshua 4:13), that Solomon kept forty thousand stalls of horses to pull his chariots (1 Kings 4:26), and that David slew forty thousand Syrian horsemen (2 Samuel 10:18) and forty thousand Syrian footmen (1 Chronicles 19:18).

"Forty" by itself simply denotes "many" in some Middle Eastern languages. Hasluck (1912–13, 221), for example, reports that in Turkish the word for forty (*kirk*) is commonly used to mean "numerous." In this way he explains certain otherwise enigmatic place names: the several rivers called Kirk Getchid ("Forty Fords"), springs called Kirk Gueuz ("Forty Eyes"), districts called Kirk In or Kirk Er ("Forty Caves"), and the town Kirk Agatch ("Forty Trees").

In Arabic and Hebrew, too, forty has the symbolic meaning of great quantity. One ethnocentric proverb shared by Jews and Arabs hinges largely on this meaning. Arabs say, "A Jew remains a Jew even after forty years," indicating simply that even after a long stretch of time one cannot expect a Jew to "mend his ways." The same is implied in the Arabic adage "Do not trust a Jew that has converted to Islam, even after forty years" (Hasan-Rokem 1982, 26). Israeli immigrants from a variety of North African and Middle Eastern backgrounds employ a number of variants of this text: from Morocco, "Do not trust the gentile even if he is forty years in the grave"; from Lebanon and Tunisia, "Do not trust the Arab(s) even after forty years in the grave"; from Egypt, "Do not trust the gentile even after forty years"; from Sephardic Palestine, "Do not trust the gentile until forty years."

There even exists an entire folktale type (AT 910*M [Aarne and Thompson 1961; Jason and Schnitzler 1970; Jason 1975]) that incorporates the same use of forty as the proverbs and almost seems designed to substantiate them at the popular level. As reproduced and discussed by Israeli folklorist Galit Hasan-Rokem (1982, 27–29) the plot is as follows:

> I. A Jewish merchant, who does not want to carry his money with him on the Sabbath, buries it in a gentile cemetery.
>
> II. The forty-years-dead non-Jew, near whose grave the money is hidden, reveals in a dream to his living relative the place of this hidden money.
>
> III. (a) The relative succeeds in getting the money, (b) the Jew is warned in a dream by his father and unearths the money in time, or (c) the gentile is told that dreams are futile, does not search for the money, and thus the money is saved.

Hasan-Rokem schematically relates a host of variations on element III of the plot, most of them collected from the Israeli Folk Archives in Haifa. Most commonly, she points out, the proverb is proved true in these tales; the narratives are thus "realizations of a figure of speech, specifically of the hyperbolic 'even forty years in his grave.' The figurative aspect" she continues, "is also stressed by the formulistic nature of the number forty. The double condition 'gentile, even forty years in the grave,' is the extreme case, meant to prove the truth of 'Do not trust the gentile' in all other, less extreme cases."

As Hasan-Rokem states elsewhere (p. 26), "The number forty is a formulaic number, widely distributed in Semitic cultures, signifying a long period." And she reports several of the many additional Middle Eastern proverbs that express this meaning of the word. For example, when Arabs say, "After forty years did the Arab take his revenge," it means that the Arab waited a long time before seeking retribution. Similarly, Palestinian Arabs declare that "the Bedouin takes revenge even after forty years and says: 'I am early!',", an ironic statement indicating, of course, that the Bedouin is quite capable of waiting a long time before seeking revenge. Palestinian Arabs also say, "The tail of the dog is crooked even after forty years in the grave"—and a variant, "The tail of the dog is crooked even after forty years in the stocks"—to refer to a person who is incapable of changing his ways, even after many long years. It is perhaps for fear of such inflexibility that Arabs proverbially warn, "The Jew does not become a Muslim but after forty generations." All of these sayings can only be understood if "forty" is taken to mean "many" or "numerous." Considering that the entire Mediterranean region has been defined as a single culture area in some important respects (e.g., Boissevain 1979; Davis 1977; Gilmore 1982; Peristiany 1965), it is not surprising that in Spain people say, "The pig has forty flavors and all of them good" (*Cuarenta sabores tiene el puerco, y todos buenos* [Rodríguez Marín 1930, 70]). Though most Muslims and Jews would probably disagree with the opinion expressed in this proverb, all could doubtless comprehend the symbolism of the number forty within it.

When speaking of the Mediterranean world in general and Spain in particular, it is difficult to avoid mentioning Francisco Franco and the fascist ideology that provided the foundation of his forty-year regime (July 1936–November 1975). His pro-natalist policy manifested itself in, among other things, an almost obsessive drive to bring the Spanish population up to forty million. As Spanish sociologist Amando de Miguel (1976, 28–39) has pointed out, the figure forty million came to have an almost magical quality under Franco. The fascist literature of the thirties, beginning with a famous text by author Ramiro Ledesma Ramos, bears primary responsibility for initiating this population policy: "We can only begin to think seriously of Spain's grandeur, and this grandeur is, in effect, only possible when the country's population shall have doubled. Forty million Spaniards inhabiting our peninsula constitute an excellent guarantee of a great economic and political — that is to say, worldwide — future" (Ledesma Ramos 1935, 93; my translation).

Franco was to reiterate this goal many times. In 1939, with his power firmly consolidated, he pronounced, "The day will arrive when our country reaches the figure of forty million inhabitants, whom it shall be able to maintain with complete dignity due to its plentiful resources" (quoted in Miguel 1976, 29; my translation). Here is just another case in which forty is equated with abundance and greatness.

FACET 2: FORTY AS A SPECIFIC QUANTITY

If forty has been commonly used as a symbolic shorthand for "many," it has also been employed at least as frequently to indicate a specific quantitative measure, be it of space, time, or money. There is abundant evidence of this usage in the Judeo-Christian tradition. Consider the Old Testament. The Flood lasted "forty days and forty nights" (Genesis 7:4); Moses was "in the mount forty days and forty nights" (Exodus 24:18); the Israelites were made to "wander in the wilderness forty years" (Numbers 14:33); Elijah went "forty days and forty nights into Horeb the mount of God" (1 Kings 19:8). It is very common in the Old Testament for reigns, be they of kings or judges, to last forty years. Hence,

David (2 Samuel 5:4), Solomon (1 Kings 11:42), and many other kings ruled for this length of time, and when Eli suddenly died of a broken neck, it was after having "judged Israel forty years" (1 Samuel 4:18). On God's instructions, Moses sent men out to search the land of Canaan for forty days (Numbers 13:25), and while the Israelites dwelt among the Canaanites, "the country was in quietness forty years" (Judges 8:28). We also frequently encounter in the Old Testament references to forty pieces of silver (e.g., Exodus 26: 19, Nehemiah 5:15) and to punishments of forty lashes (e.g., Deuteronomy 25:3). The Bible tells us that the judge Abdon had forty sons (Judges 12:14) and that a certain Hebrew temple measured forty cubits in length (1 Kings 6:17). In the Old Testament, in fact, the incidence of the number forty is probably exceeded only by that of three and seven, and counts with these as a standard unit.

It is no doubt for this reason that the number forty has acquired such importance in Jewish literary and oral traditions. The single most informative source on this matter is Louis Ginzberg's *Legends of the Jews* (1938), which cites numerous references derived from Talmudic-Midrashic literature, Tagumim literature, Haggadot, Kabbala, and other popular post-biblical commentaries. For example, it is said that Adam and Eve remained in paradise "seven days and forty years" (Ginzberg 1938, V:106), and that when the Messiah comes, his reign on earth will last forty years as well (V:183). Jewish popular tradition incorporates forty in other ways in the story of the Flood. For example, it has been said that Noah's generation became lazy and irresponsible because from a single sowing they could reap enough food to last forty years (I:152). Popular tradition also relates the forty-day Flood to "the forty days of Moses' stay on Sinai; [the Israelites] did not obey the Torah, which Moses learned in forty days, hence they were destroyed in forty days" (V:183).

The story of Moses, in fact, is filled with references to forty. The Haggada, for example, "divides the life of Moses into three equal periods. He is said to have lived forty years in Egypt, forty in Midian, and forty in the wilderness" (Ginzberg 1938, V:404). He prophesied for forty years (VI:385)—as did Jeremiah, incidentally (VI:385)—and he carried a rod that weighed forty *seim* (V:411). After he received the Ten Commandments in the wilderness, "Israel feasted for forty days" (VI:250). Legend has it, too, that while Moses led his people in the desert, a well of water followed them for forty years, "going up with them into the hills and coming down into the plains" (VI:21).

Forty years was also the length of time Rahab led an immoral life prior to her conversion (Ginzberg 1938, IV:5 and VI:171), and the time the witch of Endor practiced sorcery (VI:236). In recounting the story of David and Goliath, one version has it that Orpah, Goliath's infamous mother, accompanied her mother-in-law, Naomi, for forty steps; in exchange, Goliath was permitted to display his strength for forty days before being slain by David (IV:86).

It is not only Jewish tradition, however, that draws abundantly on forty as a chronological factor. This tendency is expressed in the other great Mediterranean religions, Christianity and Islam, as well. The Gospels of Matthew (4:2), Mark (1:13), and Luke (4:2) all speak of Jesus as having spent forty days in the desert, where he was tempted by the devil. In the development of the Christian calendar, forty-day cycles acquired inescapable prominence (Gaignebet and

Florentin 1979, 17–39). For example, the period between Christmas and Candlemas (February 2, the day marking the presentation of the infant Jesus in the Temple and of the purification of the Virgin Mary) is forty days. Candlemas (which we in the United States popularly call Groundhog Day) is, according to Roman Catholic law, the earliest permissible time for the start of Lent. In turn, Lent, lasting from Ash Wednesday to Easter, is approximately forty days, from which it derives its name in most Romance languages: in Italian, *quaresima,* from the word for forty, *quaranta*; in Spanish, *cuaresma* from *cuarenta*; in French, *carême* from *quarante*; in Catalan, *quaresma* from *quaranta.* From Easter until Ascension Day is another period of approximately forty days, for Jesus was supposed to have spent an interval of forty days on earth between his resurrection and ascension. It is this forty-day interval, in fact, that prompted Saint Augustine to declare, "I think that life itself is represented by the number forty. . . . Not without reason did the Lord remain on this earth forty days, after his resurrection, when he conversed with his disciples in this life" (quoted in Horn and Born 1975, 358).

The number forty has other sacred significances in Roman Catholicism: for example, in prayer. The Forty Hours' Devotion is above all a rite designed to honor the Blessed Sacrament. Originating from diverse medieval practices, it first took contemporary shape in sixteenth-century Milan. Originally, and during most of its existence, rules for this ceremony stipulated that members of a parish take turns offering forty hours of uninterrupted devotion, prayer, processions, and the like; churches within a single diocese could share the burden, so that when one parish ceased worshipping, the next would immediately commence until the full forty hours were completed. In the mid-nineteenth century, reforms were instituted, permitting interruption of ritual activities at night, but still requiring the forty hours of devotion in all. To explain the choice of forty hours as opposed to, say, twenty-five or fifty, it is most commonly stated that this number "signifies the approximate number of hours that our Lord's body lay in the tomb between His death and His resurrection on the third day" (Catholic University of America 1967, 1036).

The sacredness of forty also reveals itself in Christian architecture, the most startling architectural evidence coming from the now-famous Plan of St. Gall (Horn and Born 1979). St. Gall was a monastery that never actually existed but was planned according to ideal principles by a committee of leading bishops and abbots during the ninth century. Art historian Walter Horn explains that St. Gall "is not the delineation of a specific monastery but a statement of policy, that tells us of what buildings an exemplary Carolingian monastery should be comprised, and in what manner these should be laid out in relation to one another and to the whole of the monastery site" (Horn and Born 1975, 352). In other words, the plan was a realization on paper of Carolingian architectural perfection.

Given the sacred symbolism of the number, it is hardly surprising that forty should figure prominently in the plan. Not only is there a total of forty buildings, but the width of the nave of the church at St. Gall is also assigned a value of forty. Horn believes that forty was "the basis of a system of modular relationships that controls the thinking of the designing architect on all levels of planning, from the smallest constructional unit to the layout of the entire monastery site" (Horn and Born 1975, 358). It is for this reason, he says, that the number forty "holds the key position in the aesthetic organization of the Plan" (p. 383).

As further evidence of the importance of forty as a quantitative unit in Christianity, we can cite the saints known as the Forty Martyrs, whose feast day is on March 10. According to Catholic teachings, these saints were most likely forty soldiers who died in 323 A.D. at Sebaste (the modern Sivas, Turkey). For their disobedience to the Eastern Roman emperor, Licinius, who ordered them to worship idols, these men were subjected to a slow torture. It is claimed that they were exposed naked on a frozen lake in order to provide them time to repent. One of the forty soldiers did change his mind and was rescued. But another soldier, not one of the original group, declared allegiance to Christianity, replaced the apostate, and died along with his thirty-nine companions (Catholic University of America 1967, 1036–37).

F.W. Hasluck (1912–13, 226–27) relates some interesting manifestations of the cult of the Forty Martyrs of Sebaste, illustrating, as he says, "the extreme fluidity of folk tradition in such matters." In the eighteenth century, a crypt was discovered in Caesarea, Turkey, with some well-preserved bones that were attributed by Christians in the region to a group of presumed "Forty Virgin Martyrs." Says Hasluck, "We may surmise that sainthood was predicated from the preservation of the bones, the traditional number Forty from their quantity, and their sex from some accidental circumstance, such as a dream." By the early twentieth century, the sanctuary had been brought in line with orthodox teachings and was visited on the feast day of the Forty (male) Martyrs of Sebaste. On the island of Rhodes, too, there was a Church of the Forty Martyrs with a vault containing only twenty sarcophagi. Hasluck points out that this inconsistency with official religion "formed no obstacle to the pious credulity of the Rhodians, who assigned two saints to each sarcophagus."

Throughout Turkey, abandoned Christian sanctuaries devoted to the Forty Martyrs might be taken over by Muslims and either converted into a religious site devoted to forty Muslim saints or secularized by being considered a favorite haunt of forty *djinn,* or genies (Hasluck 1912–13, 227). In fact, forty as a quantitative unit is nearly as important in Islam as in Judaism and Christianity. As summarized by Hasluck, this tradition includes, in Turkey alone, "the Forty Saints on Earth, the Forty Abdals, the Forty Victims, the Forty Saints who appeared at S. Sophia, the (localized) Forty Witnesses of the El Aksa Mosque at Jerusalem, the Forty Companions of the Prophet at Damascus, the Forty Saints of Tekrit (on the Tigris), of Ramleh, and of Yoroskeui on the Bosporus; a group of forty female saints (Kirk Sultan) is worshipped near Akbaba, again on the Asiatic side of the Bosporus" (p. 223). Considering the vast importance of groups of forty saints in both Christianity and Islam, Hasluck rightly considers it difficult to decide definitively on a firm religious origin in one faith or the other for most sanctuaries (p. 225). Forty as a symbolic concept is simply too widespread and deep throughout Turkey to be attributed to anything but some common cultural substratum. In fact, as Roscher (1909, 95–100) has demonstrated, the ancient Babylonians and Mandaeans of the general region of present-day Turkey incorporated the quantity forty prominently within their ritual and belief systems. It is therefore possible that in Turkey the importance of forty represents a fusion of pre-Christian, Christian, and Muslim traditions.

Further evidence of the importance of forty throughout the Muslim world comes from anthropologist Ashraf Ghani, a native of Afghanistan. About ten miles west of Kabul, he says (personal communication), there is a shrine dedicated to the Bodies of the Forty Martyrs, in this case referring to those who brought Islam to Afghanistan in the eighth century. Tradition has it that an underground channel leads all the way from this shrine to Mecca. Throughout Afghanistan, it is thought that in order for a town to be converted into a world pilgrimage center, second only to Mecca, it would have had to house forty Muslim prophets and/or saints. In Ghani's birthplace, as in many other Afghani towns, the belief persists that only thirty-nine prophets or saints have dwelt in that particular spot. With only one more, the town would have been transformed into a magnificent pilgrimage center, claim the inhabitants.

This folk tradition is reminiscent of an Iranian joke about a rural villager who goes to the city and decides to see the movie *Ali Baba and the Forty Thieves of Baghdad*. When he asks the price of a ticket (which in American terms would be, say, $5), the ticket-seller answers that it costs $10. Aghast at this response, the villager turns away, grumbling, "I've already seen one thief [i.e., the ticket seller]. No need to see the other thirty-nine!" (Ashraf Ghani, personal communication). This joke reminds us, of course, of the story of Ali Baba, whose forty thieves are deeply entrenched within Arabic and, for more than a century now, European oral and literary traditions (e.g., Forster 1852, 591–622). The lesser-known Turkish tales collected under the title *The History of the Forty Vezirs; or, The Story of the Forty Morns and Eves* (Zāda 1886) also bear witness to the importance of the number forty in Islamic culture. Hence, there is abundant indication that in Islam, as in Judaism and Christianity, the number forty is important in and of itself as a specific quantitative unit.

FACET 3: FORTY AS SYMBOLIZING BIRTH OR RENEWAL

A third facet of forty that appears prominently in both Middle Eastern and Western culture is its signaling or symbolizing birth, whether spiritual or natural. Once again, we are confronted with forty as a sacred age or figure in Mediterranean religious traditions. When Mohammed was forty years old, for example, the archangel Gabriel is said to have appeared to him. Gabriel lured Mohammed into a cave (which perhaps explains why so many Islamic religious sites connected with forty happen to be in caves [Hasluck 1912–13]) and asked him to read. Despite his presumed illiteracy, Mohammed was able to make out the passage, "There is no God but God and Mohammed is his prophet," which is the single most important Islamic prayer. The announcement of Mohammed's religious leadership, therefore, occurred when he was forty. For him it was obviously the beginning of a new stage of life; perhaps in partial symbolization of the event, Muslims everywhere are supposed to start each day by reciting this prayer. Mohammed's spiritual transformation at age forty is thus recreated by each believer every morning, and the start of each new day becomes symbolic of spiritual rebirth.

Given this story of Mohammed's religious development, it is not surprising that some of his followers should follow a similar path. A number of well-known Islamic saints experienced turning points at age forty; this is the age, for example, when Abu Baqr was converted (Buttrick et al. 1962, 565). It is also the time when, according to the Koran (46: 14), a man is said to achieve full strength. That is, according to official Islamic doctrine, as well as in the life of its major prophet, forty is defined as the beginning of a new era of life, an era charcterized above all by maturity, be it physical or spiritual.

Traditional beliefs and practices of the Arabs reinforce the idea that forty is related to birth. One widespread legend has it that God made Adam out of clay, let him dry for forty days, and then brought him to life. Islamic folk medicine also defines the process of human conception as taking place during three consecutive forty-day intervals: during the first forty days the blood coagulates; during the second, the flesh is produced; and during the third, the soul is formed. Bodily processes in general occur in forty-day cycles, according to traditional Islamic beliefs. Hence, it is prescribed that men shave, cut their beards, and trim their nails no less frequently than every forty days. Also, since food is said to remain in the body for forty days, meat should be eaten at least that frequently; nourishment from the flesh of camels requires that these animals be fed with pure, unadulterated food during the forty days before they are slaughtered and eaten (Roscher 1909, 119–120).

69

Several of these Islamic beliefs parallel those found within Hebrew tradition. For example, the Talmud specifies that it takes forty days for the human embryo to grow, and that the process is completed on the forty-first day (Roscher 1909, 103). Ginzberg reports a rabbinical variant of this position: Adam and Eve, it is said, were created outside Paradise and entered when they were forty and eighty days old, respectively; following this development, male embryos are supposed to take forty days and female embryos eighty days to form (Ginzberg 1938, V:106). As in the case of Islam, there is evidence that the ancient Israelites, in yet another variant of the same theme, believed that the blood, the flesh, and the soul—in that order—are gradually mixed together in the process of fetal formation, and that this process takes forty days. The ancient Greeks, by the way, are also said to have shared this belief (Roscher 1909, 104), lending credence to the basically Mediterranean character of the forty syndrome.

Islamic beliefs regarding the age of maturity are also found within Hebrew tradition. Like Mohammed, key Jewish figures are said to have attained leadership capabilities and spiritual awakening at forty. Moses, we should recall, was forty years old when he led the Israelites out of Egypt. One popular version of the story of Abraham is that he recognized God at age forty (Ginzberg 1938, V:209), and it is said as well that Cain and Abel were forty years old when they offered their sacrifice (V:136). In Jewish tradition, religious and historical personages typically begin new stages of life at age forty. Isaac was forty years old when he married Rebekah (Genesis 25:20) and Esau when he married Judith (Genesis 26:34). Ishbosheth, Saul's son, began his reign as king over Israel when he was forty (2 Samuel 2:10), and Esther is said to have been the same age when she was taken to the royal court (Ginzberg 1938, VI:459).

But it is in Mediterranean folk beliefs and practices that the emphasis on change at forty seems to have exerted its greatest influence. Here forty represents not only life but also the beginning of the end of life. One of the most widely known Spanish proverbs cautions, *"De cuarenta años pa' arriba, no te mojes la barriga* (From forty years old onward, don't get your belly wet)." Like many Spanish sayings (e.g., Arora 1980; Brandes 1974), this one can be variously interpreted. Castilian informants have told me that it means that after age forty, you should bathe less frequently or that you should engage less frequently in sexual intercourse (*coitus interruptus,* the traditional birth control technique in rural Spain, produces a wet belly). A parody of this proverb warns, *"Al pasar de los cuarenta, con la cola no eches cuenta* (When you pass forty, don't count on your tail [a euphemism for phallus])." Whatever the interpretation, these sayings obviously indicate the native speakers' view that forty represents a biological turning point; upon reaching this age, one phase of life is complete and another begins.

Consider, above all, the change brought about by the forty-day postpartum recovery and purification that women in Mediterranean and Western civilizations have been subjected to for generations. Among the ancient Mandaeans and Jews, a woman was considered impure for a period of forty days after giving birth, and remained secluded during this period to avoid polluting the people around her. The same has been true traditionally among Bedouins and Arabs. Frequently, this period of seclusion terminates with some characteristic ritual; in Upper Egypt, for example, it was common practice to pour forty glasses of water over the new mother's head in the case of a male birth, and thirty glasses if the baby was a girl, in order to symbolize purification (Roscher 1909, 99–101, 118).

In Islam, a forty-day seclusion is enacted by men or women who consider themselves to possess special curing powers. In order to transform themselves into effective folk healers, these individuals refrain from speaking and from eating sweets and other delicacies during the forty days after they somehow recognize their supernatural gifts. At the end of this period, they emerge as new people, so to speak, with the ability to cure illness and to influence both benevolent and malevolent *djinn* (Ashraf Ghani, personal communication).

Although it would perhaps be impossible to trace the precise historical lines of influence, it is clear that forty-day beliefs and practices regarding birth have been transmitted to the United States. As recently as the late 1960s and early 1970s, when my daughters were born, doctors routinely recommended abstention from coitus for six weeks prior to and following parturition. Women in those days were also told that it was well to stop working six weeks before the expected delivery, and not to return until six weeks afterward. Granted, six weeks adds up to forty-two rather than an exact forty, but the correspondence is too close to be merely coincidental. In the 1980s gynecologists infrequently make such recommendations.

From the fabulously extensive and detailed American folklore collection of Newbell Niles Puckett (Hand, Casetta, and Thiederman 1981), we have excellent evidence of deeply ingrained popular beliefs associating forty days with birth. The testimonies come from European and Middle Eastern immigrants as well as from native-born Americans, demonstrating at the very least that the transmission of beliefs and practices from the Old World to the New World has probably been going on for generations, even up to our own time.

Most of the superstitions recorded by Puckett are designed not, as in Islam and ancient Judaism, to protect the general public from polluted women but rather to defend the newborn infants against harm. Hence, an Armenian woman reports that a baby must be kept in a lighted place for forty days after birth lest fairies give him or her bad luck (Hand, Casetta, and Thiederman 1981, I:138). Likewise, an Irish woman claims that a light should burn in the infant's bedroom during this period (I:25). Several informants mention beliefs that reinforce the traditional seclusion period but justify isolation of the mother and child on the grounds of their own safety. In order to avoid the effects of the evil eye, states a Persian immigrant oilman, the newborn should not be shown to anybody except close relatives during the first forty days after birth (I:133). Another Middle Easterner suggests that for the protection of mother and infant, no visitors should enter the house for forty days, and several Greek informants claim that women should not leave their houses for forty days after childbirth (I:24).

Although most of these folk beliefs were collected from people of Mediterranean background, they all came from Americans living and working in Ohio during the past half-century. The association of birth with forty is very much a part of twentieth-century American life.

FACET 4: FORTY AS TRANSITION

This brings us to the fourth and final facet of forty: its symbolic meaning as a period of recuperation, recovery, and transition from one state of being to another. As others have pointed out, in the Bible "forty days or years was the common duration of critical situations, of punishment, fasting, repentance, vigil" (Buttrick et al. 1962, 565). Hence, the stories of the Flood, of Moses on the mount, and of the Israelites wandering in the desert—which, as indicated, were said to have lasted forty days or years—incorporate critical elements of suffering and repentance. They all, too, express the situation of a people in transition, on the threshold of a new stage of existence, in which the period of abnegation produces a more purified, lawful state of being than that which existed previously. Along these lines, we might recall that forty lashes, but not more (Deuteronomy 25:3; 2 Corinthians 11:24), was a typical punishment in biblical times, and that according to Jewish legend Adam stood in the waters of the Jordan River for forty days in penance for his sin (Ginzberg 1938, I:89). In the New Testament, the forty-day fasting of Jesus in the wilderness has similar overtones. Not surprisingly, Islam shares in this tradition: Muslims believe that sinners spend forty years in Hell after death as a means to repentance (Roscher 1909, 124).

Perhaps the most common forty-day quarantine associated with purification and transition is that following a death. The ancient Egyptian process of embalming took forty days (Buttrick et al. 1962, 565), leading to a kind of spiritual rebirth as well as to supposed eternal preservation of the physical body. In Genesis 50:3 we read, in connection with Jacob's

funerary ritual in Egypt, "And forty days were fulfilled for
him; for so are fulfilled the days of those which are em-
balmed." Here we have a statement that not only reflects
the ancient Mediterranean practice of strict mourning during forty days after the death of a family member, but has
probably also perpetuated this mortuary custom through
popular adherence to biblical prescription. The Newbell
Niles Puckett collection contains information from people
of both European and Middle Eastern background that reflects a forty-day transition period after death. There are
restrictions on painting rooms and redecorating houses
(Hand, Casetta, and Thiederman 1981, II:1148, 1249) until
forty days after a family member has died. Similarly, in Islam the mourning period and family seclusion terminate
after forty days, when a large gathering is held of relatives,
neighbors, friends, and other associates of the deceased.
Those who have memorized the Koran recite it at this time;
the event signals the reentry of the mourners into society,
albeit in the altered circumstances represented by the ab-
sence of the deceased (Ashraf Ghani, personal communication).

Forty-day periods requiring seclusion, abstention, and
other restrictions are not limited to death, however. Especially in the Mediterranean world, they are initiated by a
variety of circumstances, and tend to be lumped under a
general term. At least in the Romance tongues, this term
is usually derived from the word for forty, a phenomenon
that we encountered earlier in the case of Lent. Hence, in
Italian the term *quarantena* is defined as "a kind of fast"
and "a period of segregation and observance" lasting forty
(i.e., *quaranta*) days (Istituto della Enciclopedia Italiana

1959). In Spanish the folk usage of the term *cuarentena* is the same, and also originates from the word for forty. In Catalan, the case is identical: the forty-day restrictive period is a *quarantena,* coming from forty.

What is curious, however, is that these terms refer not only to periods of precisely forty days but also to quarantines lasting various lengths of time and brought on by a diversity of circumstances. In Italian, for example, periods of recovery and disinfection yield expressions such as *una quarantena di venti, di quindici, di otto giorni ecc.,* "a quarantine of twenty, fifteen, eight days, etc." (Istituto della Enciclopedia Italiana 1959). In fact, our English word quarantine obviously derives from the Latin *quaraenta,* "forty," and also applies to periods of different lengths.

As a final, curious offshoot of forty as a symbolic representation of change we might cite a secular domain: weather prognostication. In southern Spain, for example, it is said, "If it rains on St. Vivian's Day, it will rain for forty days and a week" (*Si llueve el día de Santa Viviana, llueve cuarenta días y una semana* [Foster 1960, 61]). Such means of predicting weather were common throughout the predominantly agricultural societies of preindustrial Europe and, like so many other folk beliefs, were transmitted in a number of variants to America. Thus, it is reported that in early twentieth-century Ohio, people scrutinized the weather on any one of a variety of dates—February 2, May 1, June 8, July 15, Whitsunday, St. Edward's Day, St. Margaret's Day, All Saints' Day, Ascension Thursday, and (for Jews) Succoth—to determine what the next forty days would be like (Hand, Casetta, and Thiederman 1981, II:1470–72). One woman from Twinsburg, Ohio, even related a relevant prognosticatory verse: "St. Swithin's Day [July 15] if thou dost rain, / For forty days it will remain; / St. Swithin's Day if thou be fair, / For forty days 'twill rain nae mair." Forty-day periods thus characterize states of the weather, just like states of mourning and repentance. Like a death, the weather on a certain day may trigger a new set of circumstances, which is expected to endure for forty days.

CATEGORIZATION AND HISTORY
OF THE SYMBOL FORTY

These, then, are the four facets of forty: (1) forty as representing many; (2) forty as a self-contained unit of time and space; (3) forty as symbolizing birth or renewal; and (4) forty as signaling a period of transition. It should be evident by now that the four facets are just different aspects of more or less the same phenomenon and can hardly be separated neatly from one another. In fact, it would be difficult to treat any single item of information conveyed in this chapter as illustrating only a single facet. All the evidence I have drawn upon could easily be classified under at least two, and probably more, of the meanings of forty. Some items nicely exemplify the full four.

Consider, for example, the biblical story of the Flood. Forty here is clearly used on the literal level as a discrete period of time, thus illustrating facet 2; but on the symbolic level, all except those who follow a fundamentalist interpretation of the Bible would interpret the "forty days and forty nights" of rain to mean simply that it rained a long time, thereby manifesting facet 1. As for facet 3, forty as symbolizing birth or renewal, the Flood represented a sec-

ond chance at life. This interpretation is clear from the rep-
lication on Noah's Ark of the original human and animal
pairs, the source of world repopulation. Facet 4 is also present in the story, for it was a period of punishment and repentance, a transition from one biblical era to another. In
fact, even though the weather prognostications cited above
seem unrelated to traditions of punishment and repentance,
I suspect that because they are overwhelmingly concerned
with predicting wet and dry spells, they have their origin
in the story of the Flood. For this reason, I decided to discuss these superstitions in relation to facet 4.

And yet these traditional beliefs about the weather also
illustrate other aspects of the use of forty. They certainly exemplify forty as a discrete time unit. If we take into account
their usual association with the agricultural cycle, they might
be shown relevant to forty as a symbol of birth and renewal
as well. In the case of weather and most other examples,
then, the four-facet division must be viewed as at least somewhat artificial. As we shall see momentarily, however, this
categorization does suggest a possible cultural background
for the popular and academic theories of adult development
that were analyzed in earlier chapters.

But first, what about the origins of the cultural emphasis on forty? Very little can be said definitively. From the
occurrence and significance of forty in the three great religions of the eastern Mediterranean, one might regard this
region as the epicenter of the syndrome. The ancient Jews,
like the Babylonians and others who surrounded them, made
important use of forty in their beliefs and practices. By virtue of chronology, it may therefore have been they who transmitted this pattern to the early Christians and the Arabs.

The evidence from Turkey, however, which contains pre-Babylonian archaeological sites, indicates the possibility of an even earlier origin. It may be that the Middle East provided a point of convergence from many different secular and religious sources, all of which seemed to focus on the number forty.

From the eastern Mediterranean, it is easy to surmise how the emphasis on forty entered and diffused throughout Europe. There is, most obviously, the transmission of ideas and practices via Judeo-Christian teachings, and this is by far the most important source of its entry into the New World as well. Newbell Niles Puckett's immigrant informants were simply among the most recent generations of Christians and Jews who brought their religions, with the accompanying cultural biases, to the United States. We must not forget, however, that some of his informants were probably of Muslim background, too. Here would be an independent source, reinforcing and sustaining the importance of forty in America. Yet Muslim immigration to this country has been rather insignificant until recently, so its direct influence is probably questionable. Muslims would have exerted a stronger impact on the New World indirectly, via Europe. After all, Turkey is both European and Middle Eastern, and the Ottoman Empire ruled over much of southeastern Europe until the beginning of the twentieth century. The Moors spent eight crucial centuries on the Iberian peninsula, and engaged in long-term, intensive trade around the entire rim of the Mediterranean, especially with Italy. Thus we may consider that Muslim, Jewish, and Christian traditions have all probably merged to give the number forty uncommon significance in our own country. Since these religious traditions no doubt originally derived their emphases on forty from some common Mediterranean substratum of beliefs and practices, the relative cultural weight of one or the other on contemporary American life is more or less irrelevant.

What cannot be denied is that in the very broadest cultural terms, the number forty possesses a multifaceted symbolic significance. In the final chapters, I shall try to assess the degree to which this cultural background has or has not had an impact on theories of adult development. To conclude here, I simply wish to suggest that the four facets of forty that I have distinguished for analytical purposes correspond to the different ways in which the age forty has been treated with respect to the life course. Let us look at the analogies briefly.

(1) *Forty as symbolizing many.* This meaning is consonant with popular notions that people who are forty are old; that is, that they have accrued a large number of years.

(2) *Forty as a unit of time and space.* Relevant here is forty as a discrete unit of time, and particularly the cultural implication that forty represents wholeness or completion. This meaning is consonant with stage theories of human development posited by academic and popular psychologists, who view the years up to age forty as representing a developmental entity, "the first half of life."

(3) *Forty as indicating birth or renewal.* This meaning corresponds to ideas of what we might call self-actualization. It is at forty, we are told, that men start new families, that men and women enter new careers, that household structures change as children leave home, that opportunities present themselves for personal growth and development.

(4) *Forty as repentance, punishment, and transition.* This meaning corresponds to the very frequent notion of mid-life crisis at forty, a period of emotional agony, upheaval, and self-doubt. These feelings, according to popular ideas, frequently are symptoms of personal changes. They are growing pains, necessary for rebirth as a new and better being, and required for restoring psychological stability.

Granted, these correspondences fail to establish direct lines of causation; there is no incontrovertible scientific proof that popular and academic ideas of human development have been influenced by our general cultural background. On the other hand, given the pervasive importance of forty in religion, folklore, and other aspects of our culture, as well as the convincing symbolic relationship between the four facets of forty in the psychological and cultural domains, it would be hard to deny that some causation exists.

I prefer to put the matter more strongly. It is impossible to ignore the cultural meaning of the number forty when trying to explain the importance of the age forty in psychological monographs and in the popular mind.

XL

Having attained some understanding of the meanings of the number forty within our own and earlier cultures, and the equivalent meanings attributed to the age forty by psychologists and the general public, we now need to explore with greater specificity some of the origins of our ideas regarding adult development. In this chapter, I first wish to review some basic assumptions about life-span psychology that appear in the academic literature, and to examine briefly in what ways they are or are not valid. I then turn to the age forty and ask why it should have been assigned such a pivotal role in our developmental ideas. Finally, I try to show how the age forty has taken on different symbolic meanings during distinct historical epochs, and try to explain these changes. This final aspect of the discussion involves a consideration of the relationship between the number forty and the age forty, as well as an evaluation of the influence of culture on life crises.

LIFE-SPAN PSYCHOLOGY AS STORYTELLING

To begin, let us quickly review some of the major ideas in life-span psychology, this time applying Misia Landau's suggestion (1981) that scientific writing can be analyzed as a form of narrative literature. Narratives have been defined as "all those literary works which are distinguished by two characteristics: the presence of a story and a story-teller" (Scholes and Kellogg 1966, 4). In our case, we might say that the story is the composite or prototypical sequence of emotions, perceptions, and events that is said to characterize the lives of men and women in adulthood. The storytellers are the academic and popular psychologists, each of whom advances a unique perspective, but all of whom belong to certain schools of thought.

To the extent that these psychologists tell stories about adult development and that the stories they relate are somehow bound to particular intellectual traditions, we may consider their craft to be analogous to narrative literature. Although most of these storytellers undoubtedly see themselves as scientists, their work necessarily contains a strong humanistic, interpretive, and even artistic component. Their stories of adult development contain the three principal dimensions of narrative literature: (1) characters, in this case the prototypical men and women who advance through the stages of adulthood to death; (2) plot, which would be the way the characters progress and the nature of their experiences; and (3) theme, which, in most of the literature that we have drawn on, consists of emotional and occupational crises or transitions, and their resolution.

To analyze these three dimensions in their full richness as they appear in the life-span literature would fill a fascinating volume itself. Here I simply wish to address several aspects of the issue. Consider first Scholes and Kellogg's proposition with respect to novelists that "all art is traditional in that artists learn their craft from their predecessors to a great extent." Their elaboration of this statement (1966, 4–5) is worth citing directly:

> [Artists] begin by conceiving of the possibilities open to them in terms of the achievements they are acquainted with. They may add to the tradition, opening up new possibilities for their successors, but they begin, inevitably, with a tradition. The more aware we are — as readers, critics, or artists — of the fullness and breadth of the narrative tradition, the freer and the sounder will be the critical or artistic choices we make. For mid-twentieth-century readers a specific problem must be overcome before a balanced view of the narrative tradition becomes attainable. Something must be done about our veneration of the novel as a literary form.

It would be difficult to claim that, as a reading public, we "venerate" life-span psychology and psychologists as we do novelists, playwrights, and other creators of art. And yet it is useful to be aware that our psychological storytellers, like the fictional ones, operate according to certain explicit and implicit assumptions.

One such assumption relates to character. Anthropologists often point out that each person is partly unique, partly like some other people, and partly like all other people. In psychology, the recognition of this principle has recently received effective articulation by William McKinley Runyan (1982, 6–8), who has outlined three levels of generality in the study of lives: that which is true of individuals, that which is true of groups, and that which is true of everyone. Psychologists have obviously maintained enduring interest in individual difference and uniqueness; in fact, it is this interest that provides the bulk of Runyan's fascinating analysis of life histories and psychobiographies. However, psychologists concerned with adult development, aging, the mid-life crisis, and the like for the most part examine individual lives as prototypical of humanity in general.

To date, very little attention has been accorded to group differences in adult development. Particularly with respect to the mid-life literature, we encounter only passing references to class or ethnic differentiation, not to mention differences between ourselves and people of vastly different cultures—although recent exceptions (e.g., Brown 1982; Datan, Antonovsky, and Maoz 1981) offer hope that this situation may be changing. The one type of group variation that seems to have been examined seriously is the sexual, that between men and women (e.g., Myerhoff and Simić 1978), a phenomenon that we shall discuss a bit later. Nevertheless, the main thrust of psychological storytelling about adult development has been to seek universals, to discover what is true of all humankind. Moreover, most of the psychologists operating within this paradigm have done so implicitly.

With regard to the plot of psychological narratives about adult development, scholars and popular writers operate within a number of traditions. The one that has interested me most in this volume is what Runyan (1982, 100–118) has called the "stage-state analysis of the life course." He explains this approach as follows:

> A stage-state analysis makes the simplifying assumption that the life course can be divided into a sequence of stages and that a person can exist in one of a limited number of states within each stage. For example, if the course of early experience is divided into Freud's psychosexual stages, then individuals can be characterized according to whether they have been excessively frustrated, excessively gratified, or normally satisfied at the oral or anal stage. If the life course is divided according to Erikson's eight psychosocial stages, then persons can

presumably be characterized by their ratios of basic trust versus mistrust experienced or acquired at the oral-sensory stage, of identity versus role confusion in adolescence, intimacy versus isolation in young adulthood, and so on. In both examples, potential differences in experience can be conceptualized as possible states within relatively common stages.

The stage-state approach combines aspects of the search for common sequential order pursued in stage theories along with a concern for individual differences in the way that stages are negotiated and experienced. As expressed by Levinson et al. (1978), "Everyone lives through the same developmental periods in adulthood, just as in childhood, though people go through them in radically different ways" (p. 41).

The stage-state approach draws on a centuries-old intellectual tradition, of which the most influential psychological model builders in recent times have been Freud and Piaget. This is a tradition of which our storytellers in adult development are very much aware and with which they generally identify wholeheartedly. The part of the stage-state plot that interests me most, of course, is the standard use of forty as a divider between stages. Many of our storytellers coincide in their belief that something significant occurs to individuals at or around the age of forty.

As for the theme of our stories, it consists for the most part, and in Runyan's terms, of "the way that stages are negotiated and experienced" (1982, 101). The innumerable individual variations and adaptations that occur in this process can be subsumed under the heading "change." At least when it comes to mid-life events and experiences, the main focus of the storytellers has been on crises or transitions that are brought about by emotional growth, by internal conflicts, or by challenges and constraints presented by the outside world. Here most of our psychological storytellers are

86

probably unwitting heirs to the traditional Christian perception of adulthood, so exquisitely analyzed by historian
William Bouwsma. The "essential condition of Christian
adulthood is the capacity for growth," states Bouwsma, just
as "the worst state of man is not so much his sinfulness (for
sins can be forgiven) as the cessation of growth, arrested development, remaining fixed at any point in life" (Bouwsma
1978, 87).

We find, in psychological portrayals of life at forty, a clear
reflection of this point of view. At or about this age, people
undergo personal struggles — sometimes traumatic, sometimes not — that yield at least the possibility for the beginning of a new life, of personal development. Bouwsma (1978,
85) says that "the essential element in the Christian idea
of adulthood is . . . the capacity for growth, which is assumed
to be a potentiality of any age of life"; in this respect, the
traditional Christian view is that "the child lives on in the
man." The forty-year-old in psychological narratives does,
in fact, appear almost childlike; certainly, the analogy between this period of life and adolescence is drawn explicitly
in some of this literature. In any event, the narratives of
adulthood portray change at forty, combined with the high
possibility that if managed correctly, the problems and traumas presented to the individual at this time can be overcome. Generally, the message of our authors is optimistic.
Happiness, self-acceptance, and creative productivity await
the protagonist who is somehow able to orchestrate these
experiences to personal advantage.

This, then, is the essence of the narrative we have been
examining: mostly men, but also some women, who pass
through discrete life stages in adulthood, encounter a turn-

ing point at or about age forty, overcome the problems engendered, and convert the experience into a positive opportunity for personal growth. The characters, plot, and theme of this story have obviously enjoyed a good deal of academic and popular success. Whether or not individual men and women atually replicate the details of the story in their own lives, it is a tale that rings true, at least within our own society and culture. At the very least, it has had success at the psychological level, as a collective fantasy. And since much of the story deals with feelings rather than actions anyway, it is impossible to deny its emotional reality to the reading public. If one cannot interpret his or her own experiences in light of the tale, one can surely identify others for whom the shoe fits.

In part, the success of this story can be attributed to its ambiguity. The adjectives used to describe feelings generally provide sufficient latitude to allow everybody to identify with at least some of them. It is for this reason that the life transition in the fortieth year becomes so intriguing: it is the single explicit feature of the narrative, the one that people can actually state does or does not apply to them personally. It is also an aspect of the narrative that causes a good deal of disagreement among academic psychologists, who seem to be more interested in whether their descriptions of feelings and behavior are universally valid than in the widespread acceptance of these experiences as a collective fantasy.

IS THE STORY VALID?

Only by distinguishing two phenomena — individual feelings and experiences, on the one hand, and the culturally accepted rendition of these, on the other—are we able to answer whether and why the story we have examined is valid. At the individual level, the story is obviously true for some people and untrue for others. The existence of a life transition or crisis at or about age forty is indisputable in the lives of many artistic geniuses and ordinary people, whose biographies have been carefully scrutinized by developmental psychologists. It is difficult to generalize from these personal histories, however, because they are possibly unrepresentative. Those who fail to conform to the standard narrative tend to be screened out of what we read and hear on a daily basis.

Orville Brim (1976, 8) has advanced several effective arguments against the existence of age-linked transitions or crises in adulthood. The first is epidemiological. Brim suggests that to identify the onset of transition periods or crises, we should look to the incidence of emotional depression, which he considers to be the fundamental symptom of such life course events. True depression, he cautions, has to be distinguished from related but milder, or more ephemeral, phenomena. People of all ages, for example, suffer from sad moods during normal daily life; unlike depression, however, these moods are not incapacitating and permit individuals to carry on competently at work and home. Grief episodes, too, are characteristic at all stages of life, whenever such incidents as family deaths or unanticipated separations occur. Although emotionally wrenching, these episodes are like sad moods in that they "do not necessarily correlate with any personality change or crisis."

Real depression, by contrast, is almost always an immobilizing force in an individual's life and can frequently precipitate permanent alterations in behavior and outlook. The incidence of such depressions, says Brim, is unusually high in adolescence and mid-life. However, these life stages obviously encompass a good number of years, and depression is decidedly not associated with any one age more than another. Nor do the most common by-products of depression, like alcoholism and other forms of "self-medication," tend to cluster around any particular age in adulthood.

A second objection to the existence of age-linked crises is perhaps even more compelling, because it would be relevant to virtually all of the major symptoms, like occupational and family changes, as well as depression. Here Brim (1976, 8) is worth quoting directly:

> Clinical data and inferences from fiction or biography cannot document age links. While there certainly are many novels, many personal protocols, they are not admissible because of the missing cases. The data simply demonstrate that some males at the age of 40 report for others, or themselves, a mid-life crisis. Maybe most 40 year olds do not have this experience; maybe more 50 year olds do.

At least at the level of personal experiences, this argument is obviously valid. It explains why many Americans can identify with the mid-life crisis story, even though the one detail of a forty-year-old age link may not represent their own particular case histories. They simply transpose the overall experience to some other year, while accepting their society's version of the story as generally occurring at age forty.

Brim's arguments, while convincing at the individual level, do nothing to explain the undeniable cultural significance of age forty. For it is clear that when there is mention of age-linked changes in adulthood at all, the major transitions are overwhelmingly placed at or around age forty. It is this curious collective fantasy that requires scrutiny and that can be understood only as the combined product of a number of cultural, social, and economic circumstances.

CULTURAL UNDERPINNINGS

Let us begin with basics. We live, first of all, in a society in which both age and age grading are exceedingly important. This characteristic, which begins in childhood, was noted three decades ago by Martha Wolfenstein (1954, 103). What she pointed out at that time is no less valid today: "It is typical of American boys particularly to be intolerant of the 'kid brother' who wants to tag along and get into the big boys' game when he isn't good enough. An American boy of seven will complain that he has no one of his own age to play with; the neighbors' little boy is six. In America there tends to be a strict age-grading, which the children themselves feel strongly about."

The reason why children have such feelings, of course, is that this concern is transmitted to them by their parents, who openly seek out playmates for them within a very small age range. Throughout more than a decade of elementary and high school, the age-grade system that begins at home is solidly reinforced; one's classmates are one's age-mates, and one's friends are primarily those who are in the same school grade. Unlike people in other societies, we celebrate children's birthdays—often with considerable pomp. There is even a rule of thumb that the number of guests at a birthday party is determined by the child's age plus one. Hence, through means both subtle and direct, our children come to believe that age is important. No wonder, then, that later on it should continue to be significant, to the point that it determines marriage patterns (with wives, until recently, supposed to be younger than husbands) and residential arrangements (with some retirement communities imposing lower age limitations on membership).

We also live in a society in which quantification is highly valued. Even as I compose this essay, I am reminded daily of our obsession with counting. On the junior high school track in Berkeley where I spend nearly an hour each day jogging, men and women busily check their stopwatches and faithfully compute the laps they have run. We inject a quantitative dimension not only into our work but even into our pleasurable activities.

Nonetheless, it is probably our economic system, more than anything, that has caused us to measure our world with such assiduousness and exactitude. Our economy has made it necessary for us to count time and money (Cipolla 1967), and this preoccupation has no doubt influenced us to count ages with concern and precision. After all, the mid-life transition is said to occur when people begin counting "backward from death instead of forward from birth" (Butler 1975, 30). Our language, for better or worse, permits us to engage in such an exercise, whereas the languages of many aboriginal Australians and South American Indians, for example, are incapable of making a specific count above three or four (Tylor 1958, 240–72). Among the Kpelle of Liberia, as recently as the 1960s, there were still very few occasions for counting beyond thirty or so. Gay and Cole (1967, 42) report that one young man, a native speaker of Kpelle who had been to grade school and appeared to be of normal intelligence, "could not remember the Kpelle terms for such numbers as 73 or 238." Many Kpelle cannot solve problems involving numbers higher than thirty or forty; indeed, the word "number" is missing from the vocabulary of Kpelle adults! "It is possible to construct an artificial word *tamaa-laa*, 'many-ness,'" but this is more the invention of the linguist . . . than a term in actual use," state Gay and Cole. Only when confronted by examples like this can we recognize the pervasiveness and depth of our cultural emphasis on quantity and its potential to yield a system of age-linked life stages.

To explain the emphasis on forty as a turning point, we must consider not only the importance of quantification in our society but also our reliance on the decimal system. True, Americans have still not effected a conversion to the metric system, and we still continue to purchase baked goods by the dozen. Nonetheless, we think in units of ten, and round off to the nearest such quantity. This phenomenon is probably responsible for so-called "birthday depressions" (Scanlon 1979) in our society, as adults move from one decade to another at ages thirty, forty, and fifty. Birthday depressions are symptomatic of our system of counting; they should not, however, be considered synonymous with mid-life crises or transitions, which are, as Brim suggests (1976, 8; noted above) much more profound and enduring than are those usually associated with this relatively minor, ephemeral phenomenon.

It is the decimal system that creates the tendency to talk about, and conceive of, mid-life crises in round numbers. Following Neugarten (1972), Dorothy Rogers (1982, 118) has said that "working men may feel themselves to be middle aged at 40 and old by 60, whereas professionals and business executives may not perceive themselves as middle-aged until 50, or old until after 70." Scholars may argue about the existence of age-linked personality changes, but when they do so, they tend to anchor the discussion in terms of ages that end in zero. Ages that end in the digit five also seem to be drawn upon disproportionately, another phenomenon that follows from the decimal system. It is possible that in these practices, scholars and others are simply following the lead of their informants, who, in talking about their past lives, situate events inaccurately with reference to key ages ending in zero or five — ages that have been shown to "have a strong appeal on memory" (Acsádi and Nemeskéri 1970, 21). Equally likely, however, is that life-span psychologists themselves are affected by the decimal system and draw upon these ages as a convenient shorthand. As students in the 1960s, we believed that people over thirty could not be trusted. To whom would the ages thirty-two or twenty-seven have occurred as demarcators of trustworthiness?

These, then, are at least three of the cultural conditions that underlie our system of speaking and thinking about life stages: our emphasis on precise age, our high evaluation and use of quantification, and our reliance on the decimal system. Factors such as these are probably what explain notable differences between our view of the aging process and that of numerous non-Western, small-scale societies.

AGE-SETS IN AMERICA AND AFRICA

In a suggestive article comparing life-course transitions in the United States and sub-Saharan Africa, Anne Foner and

94

David Kertzer devise the notion of age-set to allow for cross-cultural comparisons. "The term 'age-sets,'" they say (1978, 1084), "refers to named groups of people who are assigned joint group membership as a result of their similarity in age and who proceed together at culturally prescribed intervals of transition from one age grade to another." The concept of age-set, so defined, permits cohorts in the United States, like adolescents and the elderly, to be analyzed alongside named, socially recognized age strata in societies like the Ibo of Nigeria, the Kipsigis of Kenya, the Galla of Ethiopia, and the like.

Surveying the Africanist literature, Foner and Kertzer discovered that contrary to the impression conveyed in many introductory anthropological texts, the timing of transitions from one age grade to another is often uncertain. Speaking of their African sample (1978, 1088), they state:

> According to an abstract model of the process, transitions in age-set societies occur at fixed points—say, every X years. In few societies, however, is this actually the case. Typically the timing of transitions is a product of deliberation rather than of simple chronological determination. The decision to initiate a group of young men into an age set is never made by the prospective initiates themselves. Similarly, the transition of the age set from the first grade in the system to the second grade is not decreed by the individuals making the transition. While the precise group formally controlling the decision to hold transition ceremonies differs from society to society, in 19 of the 21 societies this is the prerogative of the elders, however defined; in two societies . . . it is the prerogative of the younger age set, which occupies the position of greatest political power in the society.

How different is this system from our own! In our society, the transitions from one age grade to another occur not through the declaration or permission of any authoritative body but automatically and by virtue of common social definitions. For example, before age one we are considered "infants"; during the following year or so we are "toddlers"; between the ages of thirteen and nineteen we are "teenagers," and so on. Although our age grades are not exclusively marked in terms of absolute age, consideration of the number of years since birth would certainly be essential to any complete description of our age-set system.

When I speak of "our" age-set system, I refer above all to that which prevails in the contemporary United States. Included in this definition, however, is the implicit recognition that we share conceptions of adulthood in particular and the life course in general with other societies, especially those influenced by the Judeo-Christian tradition. The American conceptualization of the life course may be in some respects unique, but there is no doubt that it is part of a wider, historically ancient heritage that has emphasized the age forty as a turning point.

THE AGE FORTY THROUGH HISTORY

As we saw in chapter 4, the age forty was clearly a demarcator of life stages even in early biblical times. The phenomenon is particularly noteworthy in the story of Moses, whose life was transformed into a religious ideal, a model to emulate — at least among Jews and Muslims, both of whom accepted him as a prophet. However, if we wish to pinpoint a historical epoch closer to our own in time, spirit, and culture, and in which the conception of forty as a transitional age became more or less standardized, it would be the Renaissance. When Shakespeare indicated, in his second sonnet, that old age begins after "forty Winters . . . besiege thy brow," it is highly unlikely that he simply chose a random figure. His opinion was in accord with the general beliefs of his day.

We know about these beliefs thanks to Creighton Gilbert's fine essay, "When Did a Man in the Renaissance Grow Old?" (1967). Gilbert draws upon both direct and indirect statements, mostly from England and Italy, to determine that forty was indeed the beginning of old age in early modern Europe. For example, when Erasmus was forty, or just a few months short of it, he composed "On the Discomforts of Old Age"; the poem (quoted in Gilbert 1967, 11) is generally considered autobiographical, and refers to the present rather than the future. Included within it is the telling stanza:

> . . . How lately did you see this
> Fresh Erasmus blooming in mid-youth?
>   Now, quickly turning about, he
> Begins to notice the hurts of pressing old age,
>   And move toward a change,
> Unlike himself.

"On the Discomforts of Old Age" was written, incidentally, during a journey that Erasmus made to Italy in 1506. It is curious, although perhaps coincidental, that statements of life transitions seem often to coincide with trips. This phenomenon may simply indicate that authors travel a lot, or that traveling stimulates personal reflection. On the other hand, there may be some deep underlying relationship between geographic and temporal mobility, as Jung and his followers suggest (e.g., Jung 1961; Maduro 1976). In any event,

Erasmus—who was to live to seventy—clearly considered himself to have turned old at forty.

Gilbert draws further evidence from Vasari's *Lives,* which
also reflects a sixteenth-century viewpoint. In his biographies of Renaissance figures, Vasari's casual statements reveal his attitude about the ages at which they died; "deaths
before a certain age regularly include a comment that they
are untimely, and after that are neutral; at still older ages,
they may be neutral or may include a remark about advanced
years" (Gilbert 1967, 17). Through ingenious analysis of this
lengthy text, Gilbert arrives at the conclusion that "Vasari's
whole testimony is consistent with Erasmus and remarkably
consistent internally, making the sharp break [between youth
and old age] in the late thirties, perhaps the more so in being clearly a matter of habit rather than conscious notice"
(p. 19).

Gilbert's investigation of oblique or nonchalant docu-
mentary statements in many other sources yields the same
conclusion about the beginning of old age in the Renaissance. Moreover, several impressive texts that discuss the matter directly leave no doubt that forty was the conceptual
turning point. I shall cite only one, Thomas Elyot's *The Cas-
tle of Health,* a popularizing medical handbook that went
through eleven editions, starting with its initial publication
in 1534. Considering the success of this book, it is reasonable to suppose that it both reflected and influenced the
attitudes of its day. In discussing the body and its qualities,
Elyot remarks that the "Ages be foure":

> Adolescency to xxv yeres, hotte and moyst, in the whiche time
> the body groweth.

Iuventute unto xl yeres hotte and drye, wherein the bodye is
in perfyte growthe.

Senectute unto lx yeres, colde and drie, wherein the bodye be-
ginneth to decreace.

Age decrepite, until the last time of lyfe, accidently moist, but
naturally cold and dry, wherein the powers and strength of
the body be more and more minished.

Translated to contemporary English, this text (quoted in Gilbert 1967, 13) places adolescence to age twenty-five, youth
from twenty-five to forty, senescence from forty to sixty, and
decrepitude from age sixty on. Since during the Renaissance
most people stopped work and died sometime between the
ages of forty and sixty, Gilbert (1967, 13–14) perceives what
we might call a functional equivalence between this life stage
in early modern Europe and the period from sixty or sixty-
five upward today; thus, in this passage, "senectute" means
"old" as we mean it.

Although there are not reliable life-span statistics for the
Renaissance, Gilbert amasses evidence to demonstrate that
Europeans of that period, if they lived beyond early childhood, could expect to die at about fifty. This figure further
corroborates the functional equivalence of Renaissance and
contemporary points of view. In both eras, people "conceive
of the beginning of old age as a point five to ten years less
than the modal age of death, making it begin in one case
at forty and in the other at sixty-five" (Gilbert 1967, 12).
There is thus plenty of reason to believe not only that forty
was a pivotal age during the Renaissance but also that it indeed marked entry into old age. And let us not think that
this was merely a vacuous ideology without practical consequences. In Venice, for example, the Council of Ten—the

special executive body in charge of secret affairs and state security, and probably the most powerful of the city's political agencies—had a minimum age requirement of forty (Finlay 1980, 126). Since during the Renaissance "'old age' was conceived of as commencing at 40" (p. 125), it was presumably at this stage of life that men were considered to possess enough maturity and good judgment to sit on the council.

In fact, down through the centuries the wisdom that is frequently associated with old age has been anchored to the fortieth year. As long ago as the Mishnah (the collection of oral laws, classified during the second century A.D., that forms the basis of the Talmud), it was said that man begins to pursue a livelihood at twenty, reaches the peak of his strength at thirty, and attains wisdom at forty (Goldin 1957, 222). It can be no coincidence that in the mid-twentieth century, the poet Jan Struther (the *nom de plume* of Joyce Anstruther Maxtone Graham) in an autobiographical statement, seemed almost deliberately to confirm this time-honored point of view. In "All Clear" she confessed, "It took me forty years on earth / To reach this sure conclusion: / There is no Heaven but clarity, / No Hell except confusion."

THE EMERGENCE OF CONTEMPORARY AGE GRADING

How curious that right up to modern times we have evidence that the age forty has signified the onset of maturity, responsibility, and good judgment. It is mainly after World War II that the age forty takes on new meaning. Instead of symbolizing the solidity and stability that are a consequence of years of experience, forty comes to represent personal up-heaval, the reevaluation and possible destruction of a pre-viously harmonious family and occupational life, and the beginning of a new stage of existence. The mellowness and rational perspective that people in previous epochs attrib-uted to forty-year-olds now becomes postponed until later, after the mid-life crisis somehow disappears or resolves itself.

Two issues are raised by this shift: (1) why the age forty has persisted as a conceptual turning point; and (2) why the symbolic meaning of age forty has changed. The first issue is the easier to tackle because, in a sense, we have al-ready provided the explanation. The age forty has been im-portant as a turning point, and will continue to be so, be-cause of an enduring cultural heritage of which we in the United States are only among the most recent heirs. Our religious tradition defines both the number and the age forty as significant. In addition to that religious tradition and probably because of it, our language accords a special sig-nificance to the number forty. When we combine these two phenomena with our age consciousness, tendency to quan-tify, and reliance on the decimal system, it is more or less inevitable that forty should maintain its pivotal role in the conceptions that we hold of adult development.

Several factors account for changes in the meaning of the age forty. First, we should recall from chapter 4 that the number forty, symbolically considered, has a polysemic qual-ity; that is, it has a multifaceted symbolic texture. For ex-ample, it may represent, among other things, the concept of "many"; and yet this representation has either negative or positive connotations in the context of age. It could mean many in terms of "excessive," which would explain why Jack

Benny did not want to abandon being thirty-nine. Or it could mean many in terms of "sufficient," in which case it might qualify a man for political office. Each people in each historical era affected by the symbolism of forty could choose which of these potential meanings it would emphasize in its conceptualization of adult development. In the contemporary United States, we find that the transitional symbolism of the number forty is stressed in portrayals of the life course, whereas in other times and places this symbolic aspect might appear muted in the context of adult development. The number forty is like a permanent cultural resource, ready to be drawn upon and interpreted in any one of several different ways, depending upon the prevailing perspectives on adult development.

Next, we must return to our assertion in chapter 2 that there has occurred increasing age grading in the United States in the post–World War II era. Until the war, and probably for some years thereafter, age forty was viewed in the centuries-old fashion as a demarcator of old age and harbinger of imminent death. In this respect, there is very little difference between Thomas Elyot in Renaissance England and G. Stanley Hall in twentieth-century America. Only since the 1960s have we witnessed an obsession with middle age, middle adulthood, and the like. In this process, age forty has been singled out as the prime representative of these middle years.

There can be no doubt, as Tamara Hareven (1978b, 213) has observed, that we have recently witnessed socioeconomic changes that "have resulted in the segmentation of the life course into more formal stages, in more uniform and rigid transitions from one stage to the next, and in the separation of various age groups from one another." These changes have been brought about by a combination of circumstances, the most important of which are changing modes of work. Longer educational preparation for jobs and the standard-ization of retirement are just two of the important changes that have had widespread repercussions. Over recent dec-ades, communities composed entirely of "senior citizens" have grown up (Fitzgerald 1983), and the marketing of many products is increasingly geared toward particular age groups — teenagers and the elderly, for example — thereby giving these groups a phenomenological reality that they might not otherwise possess. As a result of these changes and oth-ers, like medical specialization (Katchadourian 1978), there has arisen a sharp differentiation between "middle" and "old" age, a differentiation that is historically quite recent (cf. Hareven 1978b).

The process through which age groups become socially defined, particularly in complex civilizations, is still only partially understood. French historian Philippe Ariès has probably been at the forefront of such research. In *Centuries of Childhood* (1965), he successfully demonstrated that "childhood" as a distinct social category is relatively recent in the Western world. In medieval France, for example, young human beings were not thought of as very different from older ones; hence, children were dressed like little adults and even portrayed like them artistically, with the propor-tionate size of head to body in painting and sculpture be-ing the same for all age groups. The idea of childhood as a separate stage of life developed only slowly, as children became increasingly considered a specialized category of be-ing, with their own dress, habits, games, and other activities.

In an insightful essay concerning the opposite end of the age spectrum, Frances Fitzgerald argues convincingly that "American society is creating a new category of people, called 'the aging' or 'senior citizens,' with their own distinctive habits and customs" ((1983, 54). These people—"the first generation of healthy, economically independent retired people in history" (p. 61)—have in effect created a new subculture, of which the multitudinous retirement communities that have grown up in the sun belt are the most extreme manifestation. As Fitzgerald points out, "These communities are not just places where the elderly happen to find each other, as they do in certain rural communities and certain inner-city neighborhoods after everyone else has moved out. They are deliberate creations—places where retired people have gone by choice to live with each other. Most of them, founded in the early sixties, are now old enough to have evolved from mere developers' tracts into communities with traditions of their own" (p. 65). In other words, the independent, retired elderly are now a recognizable, socially distinctive group, who arguably share certain cultural features that set them apart from other age cohorts. What earlier in history happened to childhood (and adolescence as a specialized segment of that general developmental stage) has now happened to the retirement years.

The social category of "middle age" is almost to the same point of definition, with one major exception: the economic and social circumstances that permit us to define childhood and old age chronologically have not yet produced any clearcut boundaries around middle age. Consider our contemporary notion of childhood. Childhood in the modern-day world consists, for the most part, of those years during which we are economically dependent and still preparing ourselves educationally for permanent employment. It is basically our stage of occupational development, together with our financial relationship to our parents, that determines whether or not we have left childhood and entered the adult world. With the elderly, economic forces have also played a critical defining role. Above all, standardized retirement—first at age sixty-five, but increasingly at seventy—has influenced our conception of when a person becomes a senior citizen. The combined cessation of work and financial independence are the most basic circumstances that have shaped our conception of this age group. In this regard, we should recall from chapter 3 that the Age Discrimination in Employment Act has been applied, since 1979, to people between forty and seventy years of age rather than forty and sixty-five, as was originally the case. This development, I would suggest, foreshadows a corresponding redefinition of senior citizenry in the not-too-distant future as beginning at age seventy rather than the more commonly accepted sixty-five that prevails today.

But what about the lower chronological limit to middle age? Here I believe we enter the realm of ambiguity. It is almost as if middle age, which of all the age groups in the contemporary United States is hardest to define and about which there is probably least common agreement, needed some concrete numerical representation. To fill this need, the age forty—as always, standing by as a permanent cultural resource—has been drawn upon for definitional purposes. Forty is not itself middle age, for no single year (except the first year of life, infancy) can be coterminus with an entire stage of life. Rather, forty represents—is symbolic of—middle age. To take forty as representing middle age has enabled people to situate themselves with reference to other, more clearly defined age groups. It has provided a kind of anchor point, a frame of reference, which we seem to require in the increasingly age-differentiated society in which we live. The symbolic qualities associated with the number forty also seem to have suited the personal experiences of a good number of people of the corresponding age. The transitions and new beginnings of some forty-year olds have been taken as prototypical and generalized to the age group as a whole. In this respect, our cultural heritage has operated alongside postwar economic and social transformations to alter our age-grading system; forty has become the symbol of middle rather than old age, although it retains its general significance as the demarcator of another decade along the life course.

CHAPTER SIX.

AGE FORTY AS

A CULTURAL CONSTRUCT

In the opening paragraphs of Mary Bard's memoirs, *Forty Odd* (1952, 11), the author confesses to having had what is probably a very widespread experience: "The morning of my fortieth birthday, I awoke with the same cold dread of unavoidable doom that Marie Antoinette must have felt when she awoke and knew that this was the day that she was to be guillotined." Perhaps to counteract feelings like this, the forty-year birthday party has become a familiar institution in our society. Through the elaborate celebration of children's birthdays, we unwittingly teach our sons and daughters that age is a matter for concern. Yet many of those same boys and girls may very well spend several postadolescent decades without any formal birthday celebration at all—until they reach forty, when the occasion once again becomes cause for public festivities.

How can we account for feelings such as Mary Bard's? Is the age forty actually some sort of biological turning point, or is it simply—as I have suggested throughout this volume—a cultural construct? How can we know that people undergo changes at forty not because they are genetically programmed to do so but because they are triggered by the belief that this is a precarious, transitional age? It is time now to summarize our answers to these questions, submit final evidence in support of them, and place them in theoretical context.

NATURE VERSUS NURTURE IN SAMOA

The issue that confronts us is hardly new to anthropology. As pointed out in chapter 1, debates about the nature and origin of life stages are practically as old as our discipline itself. Although recent interest in this issue has drawn on ethnographic evidence from far-flung parts of the world (e.g., Mines 1981; Fried and Fried 1980; Turnbull 1983), the greatest controversy has involved data from Samoa.

Over half a century ago, Margaret Mead, having just completed her doctoral dissertation in anthropology at Columbia University, embarked on a landmark study of female adolescence. Her task was to determine whether adolescent girls on the Polynesian island of Samoa underwent the same traumas as American girls of the same age. The more fundamental question that this information would answer was, in her own words, "Are the disturbances which vex our adolescents due to the nature of adolescence itself or to the civilisation? Under different conditions does adolescence present a different picture?" (Mead 1949, 17).

Mead's findings, reported in *Coming of Age in Samoa* (1928) and related texts, are among the most famous in all twentieth-century social science. They have been tersely and effectively summed up by her most recent critic, anthropologist Derek Freeman (1983, 93–94):

> Adolescence in Samoa, according to Mead, is . . . "peculiarly free of all those characteristics which make it a period dreaded

by adults and perilous for young people in more complex—
and often also, in more primitive[—]societies." What is the
most difficult age in American society becomes in Samoa the
age of maximum ease, "perhaps the pleasantest time the Samoan girl will ever know." With "no religious worries," "no conflicts with their parents," and "no confusion about sex" to vex
the souls of Samoan girls, their development is "smooth, un-
troubled, unstressed," and they grow up "painlessly . . . almost
unselfconsciously." And this being so, Mead states, she was left
with "just one possible conclusion": that the "woes and difficulties" of American youth could not be due to adolescence
for, as her researches had shown, in Samoa adolescence brought
"no woes." In other words, the crisis and stress of adolescence
are determined by nurture not nature.

Franz Boas, Mead's mentor and the acknowledged father of
American anthropology, declared in his foreword to her book,
"The results of her painstaking investigation confirm the
suspicion long held by anthropologists, that much of what
we ascribe to human nature is no more than a reaction to
the restraints put upon us by our civilization" (Boas 1949, 8).

Derek Freeman's critique, *Margaret Mead and Samoa: The
Making and Unmaking of an Anthropological Myth* (1983),
is the latest and certainly the longest of the commentaries
on Mead's Samoan research. Relying on published reports
from missionaries, travelers, and government documents,
as well as on his own lengthy field observations, Freeman
attempts systematically to demolish the idyllic image of that
South Sea island as created by Mead. He finds Samoan life
to be one in which a high degree of aggression and com-
petition are evident; rape and delinquency are rampant;
child rearing is traumatic; society and politics are hierarchi-
cal; and the adherence to Christianity and the virginity com-

plex are stringent. As Laura Nader has pointed out, "He draws an extreme picture of the Samoans—the *exact* opposite of the one Mead drew" (Nader 1983).

Freeman devotes a good portion of his book to tracing the history of cultural determinism in anthropology, and especially to gauging the impact on anthropological science of Franz Boas's battle against the hereditarians, who viewed beliefs and behavior as an outgrowth of biological constitution. His conclusion is that biological and cultural determinists have been at odds for too long. "The time is now conspicuously due, in both anthropology and biology," Freeman states in the final sentence of his volume, "for a synthesis in which there will be, in the study of human behavior, recognition of the radical importance of both the genetic and the exogenetic and their interaction, both in the past history of the human species and in our problematic future" (1983, 302). The inescapable implication is that a difficult period of adolescence, such as that found in Samoa and the United States, must be both biological and cultural in origin.

Nowhere in Freeman's book, however, is the evidence for a biological origin presented; as George Marcus (1983, 3) has correctly observed, Mead's critic has "nothing new to say about the relations of biology to culture." In fact, I would agree with Nader's observations (1983) that "if Mead is a cultural determinist, so too is Freeman, because the dispute is over cultural facts." Traumatic adolescence in both Samoa and the United States appears, in the end, to be caused overwhelmingly by nurture, not nature.

The most interesting feature of the Mead-Freeman debate, however—overlooked by virtually all of the recent critics

— is that both anthropologists implicitly embrace what might be called, in a terminological borrowing from human evolutionary studies, the "punctuated equilibrium" model of the life course. They implicitly view the trajectory from life to death as being made up of a series of relatively stable emotional stages, which are separated from one another by transitional crises. Mead and Freeman differ only as to whether or not such a crisis occurs during adolescence in Samoa. To repeat Nader's comment, the authors disagree about the nature of the ethnographic evidence; they overlook the more fundamental question of whether a punctuated equilibrium model of human development is viable at all, at least when applied to entire societies rather than to individuals.

In fact, a number of early critiques of Mead's Samoan research (nicely summarized in Barnouw 1973, 129–36) tried to address this very issue. It was pointed out that Mead carefully chronicled "exceptional" cases of children who did suffer a considerably traumatic adolescence; in supposedly placid Samoa, when Mead's own reported cases of mental illness were counted, their incidence in proportion to the total study population was comparable to that which would be found in the United States. It was also observed that American adolescents themselves differed substantially in their adolescent experiences: for many boys and girls, this was undoubtedly an emotionally tumultuous period, but for others it was not. Hence, critics observed, an American sample itself would have been sufficient to dismiss an organic etiology of teenage mental disturbances.

These early observations are much more telling than Freeman's because they question the very existence of regular, predictable stages in human development, whether those stages be universal or culturally specific. In the light of these criticisms, what can we say about the influence of nature and nurture in the mid-life crisis, particularly as manifested at age forty? For one thing, we can restate Orville Brim's sensible assertion that some people go through the crisis and others do not. Of those who experience it, the age at which it emerges varies widely from one individual to another. Although there is no doubt that Americans situate the crisis at or around forty in their folk and scientific conceptions of the life cycle, and that many people do experience the crisis at or around forty, the etiology of the disturbance is far from clear. For some men and women, biological changes may actually be occurring; for others, the incessant suggestions and reminders that change is supposed to occur may be sufficient to trigger it.

What is certain is that there exists no pan-human genetic program causing psychological depression, organic degeneration, or career change at forty. To demonstrate this conclusion, we can cite two important additions to the evidence already presented in this volume: first, medical testimony included in key court cases testing the Age Discrimination in Employment Act; and second, observations regarding the life cycle of women, who have only recently been defined, along with men, as experiencing a mid-life crisis at forty.

ADEA TEST CASES

Let us recall, from chapter 3, that the Age Discrimination in Employment Act of 1967 is designed specifically to protect workers of forty and older (Edelman and Siegler 1978,

255). In practical terms, this means that an individual under forty cannot claim protection under the ADEA; only if you are at least forty years old can you sue a potential employer for using age as a basis for failure to hire.

The leading test cases for the forty-year age limit are generally considered to be Hodgson v. Greyhound Lines in 1974 and Usery v. Tamiami Trail Tours in 1976, both of these being governmental lawsuits against well-known transcontinental bus companies. The two cases were occasioned by the usual industry-wide practice of refusing to hire new drivers aged forty and over. In their separate defense actions, Greyhound and Tamiami argued that because of the seniority system, new bus drivers were routinely assigned the most arduous, difficult routes. They claimed that to accept driver-applicants who were forty and older would therefore seriously affect passenger safety; passengers would be placed in the hands of drivers unable to cope with the physical demands of the job.

These cases bear on our topic because both involved careful consideration of the biological process of aging at forty. Yet a review of the decisions indicates that neither was successful in demonstrating, beyond a reasonable doubt, that forty is an organic turning point. Indeed, given the total lack of agreement on this issue, the scientific testimony seems inconclusive.

Hodgson v. Greyhound in 1974 was the result of an appeal of an earlier District Court of Illinois decision against Greyhound, in which the judge held that the bus company's maximum hiring age policy stood in violation of the ADEA. Specifically, he claimed that there was no factual basis for

Greyhound's contention that "all or substantially all [applicants over age 40] . . . would be unable to perform safely and efficiently the duties of the job involved" (Judges of the Federal Courts 1975, 861). The United States Court of Appeals reversed the Illinois decision on the basis of evidence that the "human body undergoes physical and sensory changes beginning at around age 35 and that such degenerative changes have a detrimental impact on driving skills" (p. 860). However, the same decision admitted (p. 863) that "these changes are not detectable by physical examination"! Not only does the contention that certain physical changes regularly occur at particular ages become illusory by this admission, but the case fails to include discussion of specific bodily changes at forty; only the age thirty-five is mentioned.

Usery v. Tamiami, heard in 1976, is another instance in which a District Court decision opposing bus company hiring policy was overturned by a United States Court of Appeals. In the original District Court decision, the judge concluded:

> Safety is the foremost concern involved herein not only for defendant but for plaintiff and this Court as well, but *I cannot accept the contention that persons over 40 cannot become safe bus drivers. I believe strongly that functional capacity and not chronological age ought to be the most important factor as to whether or not an individual can do a job safely.* This determination must be made repeatedly throughout the employee's employment experience. The human variances involved are myriad; there is no way to generalize as to the physical capability and physiological makeup of an individual. Nor is there a way to project how an individual will be affected by the aging process. (cited in Edelman and Siegler 1978, 103; emphasis added)

The District Court judge, in other words, rejected the notion of a standardized aging process and suggested that each applicant be evaluated on the basis of individual physical and psychological state, regardless of chronological age.

When Tamiami appealed the case, conflicting evidence was presented. In favor of the bus company was the testimony of a medical witness, Dr. Harold Brandaleone, who claimed that "while chronological age could not be isolated as a factor automatically indicating that an individual could not adjust to the rigors of the [transportation] schedule, medical science could not accurately separate chronological from functional or physiological age." Brandaleone maintained that "(1) certain physiological and psychological changes that accompany the aging process decrease the person's ability to drive safely and (2) even the most refined examinations cannot detect all of these changes. In his opinion 40 years of age was by no means an arbitrary cutoff to enable bus companies to screen out such impairments." (Judges of the Federal Court 1976, 237). And yet nothing in the report provided scientific evidence that a hiring cutoff at age forty was nonarbitrary. In fact, in one of the Greyhound decisions, we read that scientific examination is incapable of even detecting such changes as might occur at that age; a medical witness, Dr. Abraham J. Mirkin, "dismissed any relationship between age and one's ability to drive a vehicle safely" (p. 238).

Despite the contradictory statements of the witnesses, the appellate courts in both bus company cases upheld the maximum hiring age of forty. In other words, it was affirmed that for considerations of passenger safety, the Greyhound and Tamiami hiring policies could not be declared in violation of the ADEA. Throughout the testimony there is abundant recognition that the aging process is in many respects uneven and idiosyncratic, and even that it is impossible to measure. And yet forty was deemed, in the final judgment, a reasonable hiring ceiling. Reviewing these cases, Edelman and Siegler (1978, 107), esteemed legal experts on age discrimination, draw upon them to illustrate a general principle of law: "There is no mechanistic process at work but rather courts [hold] different attitudes and approaches which may lead to different results on nearly identical facts or identical results on different theories."

Here is surely an instance of how a cultural boundary—that is, our shared conception of what happens at age forty—has directly influenced millions of lives. In the case of the ADEA itself, it is difficult to say whether its legislation directly reflects cultural definitions of aging or whether the cultural definitions have produced widespread discriminatory practices in hiring, which in turn created the need for special laws to protect people over forty. Probably the ADEA application to people over forty reflects a combination of both these processes. In any event, the ADEA, by placing people over forty in a special category of employment vulnerability, has inadvertently perpetuated our cultural definitions of life stages, even though it is designed to combat such distinctions. Similarly, the Greyhound and Tamiami hiring policies both reflect and reinforce centuries-old stereotypes.

This episode in modern American history demonstrates that when legislation and personnel policy require some strict definition of the age at which full physical vigor begins to decline, they seize upon a traditional cultural resource:

forty. Laws of nurture, not nature, are what govern our conceptions of aging.

BATTLING AGE DISCRIMINATION

When humorist L. Rust Hills published *How to Retire at Forty-One* in 1973, Americans could share the author's jokes about "dropping out of the rat race without going down the drain." The economic situation at that time still seemed to permit limitless expansion; we could at least maintain the illusion that anybody who wanted a job could find one.

Now, in the 1980s, unemployment is one of the great economic problems facing the country. Demoralizing as it is for anyone to be without a job, the psychological and financial difficulties are compounded in the case of older men and women. People in this unenviable state inevitably discover firsthand the prejudices that confront older workers. It is very hard indeed for someone over forty to obtain new employment or to change careers successfully.

To tackle this problem, two large-scale voluntary associations have been founded. Both, if only by their names, are unambiguously directed toward people forty and older. The first is Forty-Plus, a loosely affiliated body of some twelve societies — ten in the United States, one in Canada, and one in England — which share more or less the same charter and goals. Each body is a locally based, voluntary, self-help association designed to provide unemployed executives with emotional support and assistance in finding jobs. In a brochure distributed to potential employers, Forty-Plus of Northern California, located in Oakland, states as part of its membership guidelines that "there are no barriers . . . as to sex, race, creed, or national origin." At a meeting of this Oakland chapter that I attended in May 1983, there was a preponderance of white males but enough minority and female participants to dispel notions that the body might be discriminatory. In fact, from items posted on the bulletin board as well as statements made during the meeting, one comes away with the impression of a very deep concern over only one particular kind of discrimination: that based on age.

To combat age discrimination, Forty-Plus members are advised of the subtle ways in which potential employers calculate age, using degree dates or precise periods of previous employment. The prevalent concern over this issue is typified in a joke circulating among the members at the time of my visit: "Did you hear what happens to you when you turn forty in Silicon Valley [the center of high-tech electronics in California, located around Santa Clara]? You turn into a microchip." People laugh at the joke, to be sure, but the sentiments and experiences that give rise to it are far from jocular for these unemployed men and women.

According to its publicity brochure, Forty-Plus has two strict membership criteria: "All [members] have earned at least $30,000 per year in an executive position and *have passed their fortieth birthdays*" (emphasis added). One informant told me that both these rules are designed to project a particular membership image to potential employers: that is, an image of highly qualified people who have reached the top of their profession. The rules also assure a certain measure of generational and economic homogeneity, which many members feel is necessary to create a supportive, cohesive group. In order to instill confidence, new members are asked to undertake a two-week initiation program that includes, among other things, listing forty accomplishments—one for each year, as a prospective member quipped—plus twenty skills that they have mastered over the course of their lifetimes. The operational methods of Forty-Plus, and its successful record as both an emotional support group and a cooperative employment agency, are fully discussed in Charles Miner's *How to Get an Executive Job after Forty* (1968). Its grateful graduates have even gone on to write self-help manuals themselves, among them *Over Forty—Out of Work? How to Win at the Job-Hunting Game* by Lou Albee (1970).

The second relevant organization is Options for Women over Forty, which also distributes a brochure clearly directed toward a particular age group. "If you're a woman over 40, you may have one-half or one-third of your life ahead of you," states the handout. As with Forty-Plus, the membership criteria for this organization are unambiguous: "OP-TIONS' members come in all sizes, shapes, colors, and ages (over 40) . . . they have just one thing in common: they are friendly women!" Although Options for Women over Forty is designed to encompass much more than career needs, a large portion of its program is geared to help, as the brochure says, "many midlife women [who] find themselves in need of a job, some for the first time due to divorce, widowhood, or some other crisis. It's not easy to enter the job market, or re-enter it, or change your career goals after many years of homemaking, but OPTIONS can help you make it." The organizers of Options clearly consider it more difficult to achieve these goals after age forty than before.

Unlike Forty-Plus, Options is strictly limited to San Francisco, although women from all over northern California have sought its services. Founded in 1978 with federal funds provided by the Community Employment and Training Act (CETA), the organization was originally called the Older Women's Project. According to Pat Durham, one of the original organizers and still active in Options, that name had inescapable negative connotations to the public at large. And many women, loath to consider themselves "older," simply turned away before they even investigated what the group had to offer. The present name, Options for Women over Forty, was then selected as the substitute because, as Durham says, forty is "the beginning of the second half of life. It is the age when one portion of your life is more or less complete" (personal communication). To some women the name is still unacceptable, testifies Durham, because they are simply unwilling ever to admit that they are over forty.

In fact, the organization does help the occasional thirty-nine-year-old woman who comes in for assistance, but if clients are younger than that, they are referred elsewhere. The goal of the organization is to help older women, those over forty, because this age cohort faces special problems of job discrimination and reduced self-esteem that are not shared by their younger sisters. The agency's statistical breakdown on clients' ages shows that 37 percent of the women who come to Options are between forty and forty-five years old. This figure is by far higher than any other single age cohort and nearly double that of the next highest group, those women forty-five to fifty, who make up 19 percent. Apparently, a great number of women between forty and fifty begin to feel discriminated against. That they come to Options for help, however, also indicates that they are optimistic about possible changes in their lives. And Options' employment record gives them good reason to be hopeful; largely because of two talented job counselors who work for the organization, over one hundred women found jobs through Options in the first half of 1983.

The very existence of Forty-Plus and Options for Women over Forty demonstrates that their members recognize the detrimental economic and psychological consequences of such culturally imposed life-stage markers as the age forty. These people also clearly refuse to accept their society's version of the aging process, because they know that physiological decline is not standardized across a population. They are like the joggers one reads about periodically (e.g., San Francisco *Chronicle*, 5 May 1983, p. 29; 10 October 1983; p. 44), who achieve their greatest feats during their fortieth year. To be sure, nature imposes limitations, but nurture undoubtedly influences the pace at which we choose to capitulate to them.

WOMEN REDEFINED

The founding of Options for Women over Forty is symptomatic of a profound change in our perception of women. The forty-year-old demarcator until recently applied only to men, but society's conception of the female life cycle is beginning to approximate that of the male life cycle. This redefinition process has made age forty a more significant boundary for women now than it was in the past.

In a justly celebrated paper published over a decade ago, Sherry Ortner (1974) argues that there is a universal tendency to conceive of men as close to culture and women as close to nature. Ortner dismisses outright the absurd proposition that women might in reality be any closer to or further from nature than man; as she says, "both have consciousness, both are mortal" (p. 87). But there is no doubt that owing partly to the woman's "greater bodily involvement with the natural functions surrounding reproduction" (p. 76) and partly to her "close association with the domestic context" (p. 78), she is seen as more a part of nature than man is. Other researchers (e.g., Ardener 1975; Barnes 1973; Mathieu 1973) have echoed and elaborated on this insight. But how does the alignment of men with culture and women with nature affect our shared images and application of the age forty?

The answer is simply that the age forty—as a cultural rather than a biological boundary—has been most consistently applied to men, at least in the American context. When academic and popular psychologists began writing about the mid-life crisis and situating this event at or about age forty, it was mainly (if not exclusively) males that they were talking about. Sexual upheavals, occupational transitions, family breakups—these and other similar phenomena were, throughout the 1960s and into the early 1970s, attributed mainly to changes that were going on inside of men. Even when women wrote about the mid-life crisis—Barbara Fried (1967) is just one example—the main subjects of their discussion were the males of the species. Problems of middle age, to be sure, have been discussed in the literature with reference to women, but with few exceptions these studies have focused on family role changes in mid-life that affect women in different cultures or, significantly, on the psychological response to menopause (e.g., Brown 1982; Datan, Antonovsky, and Maoz 1981).

Perhaps the earliest departure from this pattern was Jules Henry's highly innovative essay, "Forty-Year-Old Jitters in

Married Urban Women," first prepared in 1965 and reprinted several times, throughout the 1970s. This article surely represents one of the first clear statements of a mid-life crisis among forty-year-old women, yet as an early statement, it still reflects some of the more traditional views of middle-aged women. We read, for example, that women undergo menopause around age forty, and since they tend to over-value fertility, this change of life induces depression (Henry 1973, 141). We also read about the well-known empty-nest syndrome, the crisis supposedly brought on by "the loss of maternal functions" (pp. 139–40). Further, Henry says, women at forty are victimized by the fact that their husbands may "turn to a young and pretty woman for comfort and reassurance" at a time when the wives themselves are growing "big-bellied, heavy-breasted, fat-hipped" (pp. 137, 144). All of these presumed causes for the "jitters" are perceived in terms of natural function: woman as procreator, woman as mother, woman as siren. But Henry is unusual in that he ties these problems to a cultural marker, the age forty. His words remind us of that self-disparaging description one used to hear women give of themselves: "fair, fat, and forty."

Since the 1970s and increasingly into the 1980s, the feminist movement, and especially the involvement of women in professional careers on a par with men, has produced a redefinition of females. Noticeably, their life course has been more frequently described by cultural demarcators, and their dependency on natural functions has become steadily more muted in psychological and cultural accounts. Now, when we read about the impact of menopause, it is likely to be viewed as a liberating rather than a regrettable event. In a study of women from five different Israeli subcultures, Nancy Datan reports that "women in all cultures responded positively to questions about the loss of fertility at menopause" (Datan, Antonovsky, and Maoz, 1981, 112). This finding is consonant with that of the cross-cultural literature reviewed recently by Judith Brown (1982). The present trend is to portray menopausal women as feeling freed from the shackles of reproductive biorhythms.

Correspondingly, women have been blanketed in to the more culturally determined life-course transitions, specifically to that which is supposed to occur at age forty. Thus we have Janet Harris writing about *The Prime of Ms. America: The American Woman at Forty* (1975) and Ruth Harriet Jacobs publishing *Life after Youth: Female, Forty—What Next?* (1979). As women have made strides toward social and economic equality, so too they have earned the dubious privilege of being affected by the same culturally induced psychological syndromes as men. To be sure, the process of redefinition has been uneven and incomplete. As recently as 1983, a well-known female life-span social psychologist chuckled when I described my research on age forty. "Are you forty?" she asked, and when I assented, she added, "Why is it that you men are always interested in forty? It doesn't mean anything to us women, you know." Her testimony was a reflection of traditional circumstances. As a cultural demarcator, the age forty has been used more often to define men's progression through the life course than that of women. To this extent, it has possibly induced more men than women into a mid-life crisis at this age, although the impact on both sexes since the 1970s has no doubt become equalized in this respect.

124

SUMMARY CONCLUSION

The mid-life crisis, like the crisis of adolescence, is a cultural construct that becomes more true and more real as the
notion of its existence becomes more widely disseminated
and accepted. In a society like our own, the age forty has
become a time when we can predict trouble. We are told
over and over, in ways both subtle and overt, that trouble
will come—and so it does. The age forty provides us with
a way of interpreting irrational feelings and behavior in ourselves and others. Our cultural heritage and economic circumstances reinforce the significance of forty, and so, like
adolescence, it becomes a time of life when we are expected
—even encouraged—to let loose and go a little crazy. The
experience may seem biological because we think of it as
natural, but it is actually our culture that defines it for us
and thereby helps to produce it.

In this connection, we must keep in mind that we are
a reading public. Our culture is transmitted not only orally,
as has been the case in all societies throughout history, but
also and very importantly through the written word. There
is abundant evidence that academic psychologists, popular
psychologists, journalists, travelers, and others all reinforce
our cultural predisposition to conceive of forty as a landmark year. We receive constant if subtle reminders that our
fortieth birthday is or should be of some unusual import.

In discussing a similar phenomenon, historian Winthrop
Jordan quotes from a recent newspaper article entitled,
"Transitions: How Adults Cope with Change." The article
reads: "Adults don't stay put the way they used to. Everywhere you look, people are moving around, changing jobs,

going back to school, getting divorced. Starting over, in short. At age 30, 40, 50, 60 — there's no end to it" (quoted in Jordan 1978, 197). Jordan's comment on this piece reflects my own point of view: "In such remarks we sense not only a description of real events but an endorsement of them. We also sense that without such endorsements the events would not be taking place." In other words, the expectation of change at certain key times along the life course — especially if such expectation is elevated to the position of a shared, transmitted cultural norm — is likely actually to produce a change that might not otherwise occur.

It is possible that with increased longevity, the meaning of forty will itself evolve. For centuries, it signaled the onset of old age and was perceived as a harbinger of death. Later, it came to represent middle age and symbolized a kind of last chance at personal transformation. In time, if humans begin living long enough and if the socioeconomic circumstances are propitious, forty may assume the significance that adolescence now holds for us. Only the future can tell whether this symbolic redefinition will come to pass. What is certain is that barring some unforeseen cultural cataclysm, the number forty and the age forty will long continue to evoke highly charged associations. The history of Western number symbolism and social thought pretty well assures the perpetuation of this long-standing tradition.

Aarne, Antti, and Stith Thompson
1961   *The Types of the Folktale: A Classification and Bibliography.* 2d rev. Helsinki: Suomalainen Tiedeakatemia.

Abbot, A.E.
1962   *The Number Three: Its Occult Significance in Human Life.* London: Emerson.

Acsádi, G., and J. Nemeskéri
1970   *History of Human Life-Span and Mortality.* Budapest: Akadémiai Kiadó.

Albee, Lou
1970   *Over Forty — Out of Work? How to Win at the Job-Hunting Game.* Englewood Cliffs, N.J.: Prentice-Hall.

Ardener, Edwin
1975   Belief and the problem of women. In *Perceiving Women,* ed. Shirley Ardener, 1–28. New York: Wiley.

Ariès, Philippe
1965   *Centuries of Childhood.* Trans. Robert Baldick. New York: Random House.

Arora, Shirley
1980   "To the grave with the dead . . .": Ambivalence in a Spanish Proverb. *Fabula* 21:223–46.

Baltes, Paul B., and Sherry L. Willis

1979   Life-Span Developmental Psychology, Cognitive Functioning, and Social Policy. In *Aging from Birth to Death,* ed. Matilda White Riley, 15–46. Boulder, Colo.: Westview.

Barber, Cesar Lombardi

1959   *Shakespeare's Festive Comedy: A Study of Dramatic Form and Its Relation to Social Custom.* Princeton: Princeton Univ. Press.

Bard, Mary

1952   *Forty Odd.* Philadelphia: Lippincott.

Barnes, John A.

1973   Genetrix: genitor:: Nature: culture? In *The Character of Kinship,* ed. J. Goody, 61–74. Cambridge: Cambridge Univ. Press.

Barnouw, Victor

1973   *Culture and Personality.* Rev. ed. Homewood, Ill.: Dorsey.

Begley, Sharon

1983   The Myths of Middle Age. *Newsweek,* 14 Feb., pp. 73, 75.

Ben Cheneb, Mohammed

1926   Du nombre trois chez les Arabes. *Revue Africaine* 67:105–78.

Bennett, Alan

1969   *Forty Years On.* London: Faber and Faber.

Berreman, Gerald D.

1972   *Hindus of the Himalayas: Ethnography and Change.* Berkeley: Univ. of California Press.

Blanda, George, with Mickey Herskowitz

1978   *Over Forty: Feeling Great and Looking Good!* New York: Simon and Schuster.

Boas, Franz

1949   Foreword to Margaret Mead, *Coming of Age of Samoa,* 1–13. New York: Morrow.

Boissevain, Jeremy

1979   Towards a Social Anthropology of the Mediterranean. *Current Anthropology* 20 (1): 81–94.

Bouwsma, William

1978   Christian Adulthood. In *Adulthood,* ed. Erik H. Erikson, 81–96. New York: Norton.

Brandes, Stanley

1974   The Selection Process in Proverb Use: A Spanish Example. *Southern Folklore Quarterly* 38 (3): 167–86.

1975   *Migration, Kinship, and Community: Tradition and Transition in a Spanish Village.* New York: Academic Press.

1980   *Metaphors of Masculinity: Sex and Status in Andalusian Folklore.* Philadelphia: Univ. of Pennsylvania Press.

Brim, Orville, Jr.

1976   Theories of the Male Mid-Life Crisis. *Counseling Psychologist* 6:2–9.

Brough, J.

1959   The Tripartite Ideology of the Indo-Europeans: An Experiment in Method. *Bulletin of the School of Oriental and African Studies* 22:69–95.

Brown, Judith K.

1982 Cross-cultural Perspectives on Middle-Aged Women. *Current Anthropology* 23 (2): 143–56.

Buckland, A.W.

1895 Four, as a Sacred Number. *Journal of the Anthropological Institute* 25:96–102.

Bühler, Charlotte

1968 The Course of Human Life as a Psychological Problem. *Human Development* 11:184–200.

Butler, R.N.

1975 *Why Survive? Being Old in America.* New York: Harper and Row.

Buttrick, George Arthur, Thomas Samuel Kepler, John Knox, Herbert Gordon May, and Samuel Terrien

1962 *The Interpreter's Dictionary of the Bible,* vol. 3. New York: Abingdon Press.

Cain, Leonard D.

1964 Life Course and Social Structure. In *Handbook of Modern Sociology,* ed. R.E.L. Farris, 272–309. Chicago: Rand McNally.

Catholic University of America Editorial Staff, ed.

1967 *New Catholic Encyclopedia,* vol. 5. New York: McGraw-Hill.

Charles, Don C.

1970 Historical Antecedents of Life-Span Developmental Psychology. In *Life-Span Developmental Psychology: Psychological Research and Theory,* ed. L.R. Goulet and Paul B. Baltes, 23–52. New York: Academic Press.

Cipolla, Carlo M.

1967 *Clocks and Culture, 1300–1700.* London: Collins.

References Cited

Clausen, John

1972 The Life Course of Individuals. In *Aging and Society: A Sociology of Age Stratification,* vol. 3, ed. Matilda White Riley, Marilyn Johnson, and Anne Foner, 457–514. New York: Russell Sage.

Colson, Elizabeth

1977 The Least Common Denominator. In *Secular Ritual,* ed. Sally F. Moore and Barbara G. Myerhoff, 189–98. Assen/Amsterdam: Van Gorcum.

Craigie, Sir William A., and James R. Hulbert, eds.

1940 *A Dictionary of American English on Historical Principles,* vol. 2. Chicago: Univ. of Chicago Press.

Datan, Nancy, Aaron Antonovsky, and Benjamin Maoz

1981 *A Time to Reap: The Middle Age of Women in Five Israeli Subcultures.* Baltimore, Md.: Johns Hopkins Univ. Press.

Davis, John

1977 *People of the Mediterranean: An Essay in Comparative Social Anthropology.* London: Routledge & Kegan Paul.

Davitz, Joel, and Lois Davitz

1976 *Making It from 40 to 50.* New York: Random House.

Deonna, W.

1954 Trois, superlatif absolu. *L'antiquité classique* 23: 403–28.

Dreiser, Theodore

1914 *A Traveler at Forty.* New York: Century.

Dublin, Louis I., Alfred J. Lotka, and Mortimer Spiegelman

1949 *Length of Life: A Study of the Life Table.* New York: Ronald Press.

Dumézil, Georges

1958   *L'idéologie tripartite des Indo-Européens*. Brussels: Collection Latomus, no. 31.

Dundes, Alan

1978a "To love my father all": A Psychoanalytic Study of the Folktale Source of King Lear. In *Essays in Folkloristics*, 207–22. Meerut, India: Folklore Institute.

1978b The Number Three in American Culture. In *Essays in Folkloristics*, 129–58. Meerut, India: Folklore Institute.

Edelman, Charles D., and Ilene C. Siegler

1978   *Federal Age Discrimination in Employment Law: Slowing Down the Gold Watch*. Charlottesville, Va.: Michie.

Erben, Karel Jaromir

1857   O dvojici a o trojici v bàjeslovi slvanskèm (About the number two and the number three in Slavic mythology). *Casopis Musea Kralovstvi Ceskeho* 31:268–86, 390–415.

Erikson, Erik H.

1963   *Childhood and Society*. 2d ed. New York: Norton.

Federal Regulation of Employment Service

1981   *Job Discrimination*. Rochester, N.Y.: Lawyers' Cooperative.

Ferro-Luzzi, Gabriella Eichinger

1974   Women's Pollution Periods in Tamilnad (India). *Anthropos* 69:113–61.

References Cited

Finlay, Robert
1980   *Politics in Renaissance Venice.* New Brunswick, N.J.:
        Rutgers Univ. Press.

Fitzgerald, Frances
1983   A Reporter at Large: Interlude. *New Yorker,* April 25,
        pp. 54–109.

Flavell, John
1977   *Cognitive Development.* Englewood Cliffs, N.J.:
        Prentice-Hall.

Foner, Anne, and David Kertzer
1978   Transitions over the Life Course: Lessons from Age-
        set Societies. *American Journal of Sociology* 83 (5):
        1081–1104.

Forster, Edward, trans.
1852   *The Arabian Nights' Entertainments.* London: Wil-
        loughby.

Foster, George M.
1960   *Culture and Conquest: America's Spanish Heritage.*
        Viking Fund Publications in Anthropology, no. 27.
        New York: Wenner-Gren Foundation.

Freeman, Derek
1983   *Margaret Mead and Samoa: The Making and Un-
        making of an Anthropological Myth.* Cambridge,
        Mass.: Harvard Univ. Press.

Fried, Barbara
1967   *The Middle-Age Crisis.* New York: Harper & Row.

Fried, Martha Nemes, and Morton H. Fried
1980   *Transitions: Four Rituals in Eight Cultures.* New York: Norton.

Fry, Christine L.
1976   The Ages of Adulthood: A Question of Numbers. *Journal of Gerontology* 31:170–77.

Gaignebet, Claude, and Marie-Claude Florentin
1979   *Le carnaval: Essais de mythologie populaire.* Paris: Payot.

Garchik, Leah
1982   Interview [with] P.D. James. *San Francisco Chronicle,* October 24, rev. sec., p. 11.

Gardner, Howard
1982   *Developmental Psychology.* 2d ed. Boston: Little, Brown.

Gay, John, and Michael Cole
1967   *The New Mathematics and an Old Culture: A Study of Learning among the Kpelle of Liberia.* New York: Holt, Rinehart, & Winston.

Geil, William Edgar
1926   *The Sacred 5 of China.* Boston: Houghton Mifflin.

Gilbert, Conrad Miller
1948   *We Over Forty: America's Human Scrap Pile.* Philadelphia: Westbrook.

Gilbert, Creighton
1967   When Did a Man in the Renaissance Grow Old? *Studies in the Renaissance* 14:7–32.

Gilmore, David D.

1982 Anthropology of the Mediterranean Area. *Annual Reviews in Anthropology* 11:175–205.

Ginzberg, Louis

1938 *Legends of the Jews.* 7 vols. Philadelphia: Jewish Publications Society of America.

Glenn, Jules

1965 Sensory Determinants of the Symbol Three. *Journal of the American Psychoanalytic Association* 13:422–34.

Glick, P.C., and R. Parke, Jr.

1965 New Approaches in Studying the Life Cycle of the Family. *Demography* 2:187–202.

Goldin, Judah, ed.

1957 *The Living Talmud: The Wisdom of Its Fathers and Its Classical Commentaries.* New York: Mentor.

Goodrich, Lloyd, and Edward Bryant

1962 *Forty Artists under Forty, from the Collection of the Whitney Museum of American Art.* New York: Praeger.

Goudy, Henry

1910 *Trichotomy in Roman Law.* Oxford: Clarendon Press.

Gould, Roger L.

1978 *Transformations: Growth and Change in Adult Life.* New York: Simon & Schuster.

Gunther, R.F.

1912 Worauf Beruht die Vorherrschaft der Drei in Menschen? *Nord und Sud* 142:313–25.

Hall, G. Stanley

1904   *Adolescence.* New York: Appleton.

1922   *Senescence: The Last Half of Life.* New York: Appleton.

Hammel, E.A.

1983   *The Productivity of Chemists and Mathematicians at the University of California: An Age/Cohort Analysis.* Program in Population Research, Working Paper no. 10. Berkeley: Univ. of California.

Hand, Wayland D., Anna Casetta, and Sondra B. Thiederman, eds.

1981   *Popular Beliefs and Superstititions: A Compendium of American Folklore from the Ohio Collection of Newball Niles Puckett.* 3 vols. Boston: G.K. Hall.

Hareven, Tamara K.

1978a   The Historical Study of the Life Course. In *Transitions: The Family and the Life Course in Historical Perspective,* ed. Tamara K. Hareven, 1–16. New York: Academic Press.

1978b   The Last Stage. In *Adulthood,* ed. Erik H. Erikson, 201–16. New York: Norton.

Harris, Janet

1975   *The Prime of Ms. America: The American Woman at Forty.* New York: Putnam.

Hasan-Rokem, Galit

1982   *Proverbs in Israeli Folk Narratives: A Structural Semantic Analysis.* Folklore Fellows Communications, no. 232. Helsinki: Suomalainen Tiedeakatemia.

Hasluck, F.W.

1912   The Forty. *Annual of the British School at Athens*
−13   19:221–28.

Heizer, Robert F.

1962 The Background of Thomsen's Three-Age System. *Technology and Culture* 3:259–66.

Henry, Jules

1973 Forty-Year-Old Jitters in Married Urban Women. In *On Sham, Vulnerability, and Other Forms of Self-Destruction*, 128–48. London: Penguin.

Hills, L. Rust

1973 *How to Retire at Forty-One; or, Dropping Out of the Rat Race without Going Down the Drain.* New York: Doubleday.

Honzik, M.P., and J.W. MacFarlane

1973 Personality Development and Intellectual Functioning from 21 Months to 40 Years. In *Intellectual Functioning in Adults*, ed. L.F. Jarvik, C. Eisdorfer, J.E. Blum, 45–58. New York: Springer.

Horn, Walter, and Ernest Born

1975 On the Selective Use of Sacred Numbers and the Creation in Carolingian Architecture of a new Aesthetic Based on Modular Concepts. *Viator: Medieval and Renaissance Studies* 6:351–90.

1979 *The Plan of St. Gall: A Study of the Architecture and Economy of Life in a Paradigmatic Carolingian Monastery.* Berkeley: Univ. of California Press.

Hunt, Bernice, and Morton Hunt

1975 *Prime Time: A Guide to the Pleasures and Opportunities of the New Middle Age.* New York: Stein & Day.

Istituto della Enciclopedia Italiana

1959 *Dizionario Enciclopedico Italiano.* Rome: Istituto della Enciclopedia Italiana.

Jacobs, Ruth Harriet

1979   *Life after Youth: Female, Forty—What Next?* Boston: Beacon.

Jaques, Elliott

1965   Death and the Mid-Life Crisis. *International Journal of Psychoanalysis* 46:502–14.

Jason, Heda

1975   *Types of Oral Tales in Israel.* Part II. Jerusalem: Israel Ethnographic Society.

Jason, Heda, and Otto Schnitzler

1970   The Eberhard-Boratav Index of Turkish Folktales in the New Revision of Aarne-Thompson's Types of the Folktale. *Folklore Research Center Studies* (Jerusalem) 1:43–71.

Jordan, Winthrop D.

1978   Searching for Adulthood in America. In *Adulthood,* ed. Erik H. Erikson, 189–99. New York: Norton.

Judges of the Federal Courts

1975   *Federal Reporter.* 2d ser., vol. 499, pp. 859–65. St. Paul, Minn.: West.

1976   *Federal Reporter.* 2d ser., vol. 531, pp. 224–48. St. Paul, Minn.: West.

Jung, Carl G.

1961   *Memories, Dreams, Reflections.* Trans. Richard Winston and Clara Winston. New York: Vintage.

1969   The Stages of Life. 1931. Trans. R.F.C. Hall. In *The Structure and Dynamics of the Psyche,* 387–403. Princeton, N.J.: Princeton Univ. Press.

Kakutani, Michiko
1983   Scorsese: The King of Americana Themes. *San Francisco Chronicle,* 13 March, Datebook pp. 17, 26.

Katchadourian, Herant A.
1978   Medical Perspectives on Adulthood. In *Adulthood,* ed. Erik H. Erikson. New York: Norton.

Kertzer, David I., and Jennie Keith, eds.
1984   *Age and Anthropological Theory.* Ithaca, N.Y.: Cornell Univ. Press.

Kimbrough, Emily
1954   *Forty Plus and Fancy Free.* New York: Harper.

LaBouvie-Vief, G.
1980   Beyond Formal Operations: Uses and Limits of Pure Logic in Life-Span Development. *Human Development* 23:141–61.

Landau, Misia Lipschutz
1981   The Anthropogenic: Paleoanthropological Writing as a Genre of Literature. Ph.D. diss. Yale University.

La Sorsa, Saverio
1963   Il numero 3 nella terapia populare. *Annali di Medicina Navale* 68:171–74.

Lear, Martha Weinman
1973   Is There a Male Menopause? *New York Times Magazine,* 28 Jan., pp. 10–11, 61.

Lease, Emory B.
1919   The Number Three, Mysterious, Mystic, Magic. *Classical Philology* 14:56–73.

Ledesma Ramos, Ramiro

1935 *Discurso a las juventudes de España.* Madrid: Tecnos.

Lehmann, Alfred

1914 *Dreiheit und dreifache Wiederholung im deutschen Volksmärchen.* Leipzig: Robert Noske.

LeVine, Robert

1980 Adulthood among the Gusii of Kenya. In *Themes of Work and Love in Adulthood,* ed. Neil J. Smelser and Erik H. Erikson, 77–104. Cambridge, Mass.: Harvard Univ. Press.

Levinson, Daniel J., with Charlotte N. Darrow, Edward B. Klein, Maria H. Levinson, and Braxton McKee

1978 *The Seasons of a Man's Life.* New York: Ballantine.

Linden, M.E., and D. Courtney

1953 The Human Life Cycle and its Interruptions. *American Journal of Psychiatry* 109:906–15.

London, Michael

1982 Rolling Cameras for Mick Jagger. *San Francisco Chronicle,* 7 Nov., Datebook, p. 27.

Lopata, Helena Znaniecki

1975 Widowhood: Societal Factors in Life-Span Disruptions and Alternatives. In *Life-Span Developmental Psychology: Normative Life Crises,* ed. Nancy Datan and Leon H. Ginsberg, 217–34. New York: Academic Press.

1980 The Widowed Family Member. In *Transitions of Aging,* ed. Nancy Datan and Nancy Lohmann, 93–118. New York: Academic Press.

Lowenthal, Marjorie Fiske, Majda Thurnher, David Chiri-
    boga, et al.

1975   *Four Stages of Life: A Comparative Study of Women
        and Men Facing Transitions.* San Francisco: Jossey-Bass.

Lowie, Robert H.

1925   Five as a Mystic Number. *American Anthropologist*
        27:578.

McGill, Michael

1980   *The 40–60 Year Old Male.* New York: Simon &
        Schuster.

McMorrow, Fred

1974   *Midolesence: The Dangerous Years.* New York: Quad-
        rangle.

Maduro, Reynaldo

1976   Journey Dreams in Latino Group Psychotherapy. *Psy-
        chotherapy: Theory, Research, and Practice* 13:148–55.

Marcus, George E.

1983   One Man's Mead. *New York Times Book Review,* 27
        March, pp. 3, 22, 24.

Mathews, Mitford M.

1951   *A Dictionary of Americanisms on Historical Princi-
        ples,* vol. 1. Chicago: Univ. of Chicago Press.

Mathieu, N.C.

1973   Homme-culture, femme-nature? *L'Homme* (July–
        Sept.): 101–13.

Mayer, Nancy

1978   *The Male Mid-Life Crisis: Fresh Starts after 40.* New
        York: Signet.

Mead, Margaret

1949   *Coming of Age in Samoa.* 1928. New York: Morrow.

Miguel, Amando de

1976   *Cuarenta millones de españoles cuarenta años después.* Barcelona: Grijalbo.

Miner, Charles

1968   *How to Get an Executive Job after 40.* New York: Collier.

Mines, Mattison

1981   Indian Transitions: A Comparative Analysis of Adult Stages of Development. *Ethos* 9:95–121.

Murray, Sir James A. Henry, ed.

1933   *Oxford English Dictionary,* vol. 4. Oxford: Clarendon.

Myerhoff, Barbara G., and Andrei Simić, eds.

1978   *Life's Career—Aging: Cultural Variations on Growing Old.* Beverly Hills, Calif.: Sage.

Nader, Laura

1983   Review of *Margaret Mead and Samoa,* by Derek Freeman. *Los Angeles Times Book Review,* 10 April.

Neugarten, Bernice L.

1972   Personality and the aging process. *Gerontologist* 12: 9–15.

Ortner, Sherry B.

1974   Is female to male as nature is to culture? In *Woman, Culture, and Society,* ed. Michelle Z. Rosaldo and Louise Lamphere, 67–88. Stanford, Calif.: Stanford Univ. Press.

Osler, William
1905 Valedictory Address at Johns Hopkins University. *Journal of the American Medical Association* 44:705–10.

Paine, Levi Leonard
1901 *The Ethnic Trinities and Their Relations to the Christian Trinity.* Boston: Houghton Mifflin.

Parsons, Elsie Clews
1916 The Favorite Number of the Zuñi. *Scientific Monthly* 3:596–600.

Partridge, Eric
1949 *A Dictionary of the Underworld.* London: Routledge & Kegan Paul.
1961a *A Dictionary of Slang and Unconventional English.* New York: Macmillan.
1961b *A Dictionary of Slang and Unconventional English,* vol. 2, Supplement. London: Routledge & Kegan Paul.

Peristiany, J.G., ed.
1965 *Honour and Shame: The Values of Mediterranean Society.* London: Weidenfeld & Nicolson.

Peterson, Robert
1967 *New Life Begins at Forty.* New York: Trident.

Pitkin, Walter B.
1932 *Life Begins at Forty.* New York: McGraw-Hill.

Propp, Vladimir
1958 Morphology of the Folktale. Trans. Laurence Scott. *International Journal of American Linguistics* 24 (4): pt. 3.

Purtell, Thelma C.
1963   *Generation in the Middle.* New York: Eriksson.

Riegel, Klaus F.
1975   Adult Life Crises: A Dialectic Interpretation of Development. In *Life-Span Developmental Psychology,* ed. Nancy Datan and Leon H. Ginsberg, 99–128. New York: Academic Press.

Riley, Matilda White, ed.
1979   *Aging from Birth to Death: Interdisciplinary Perspectives.* Boulder, Colo.: Westview.

Rodríguez Marín, Francisco
1930   *12.600 Refranes más, no contenidos en la colección del Maestro Gonzalo Correas ni en "Más de 21.000 refranes castellanos."* Madrid: Festina Lente.

Rogers, Dorothy
1982   *The Adult Years: An Introduction to Aging.* 2d ed. Englewood Cliffs, N.J.: Prentice-Hall.

Roscher, Wilhelm Heinrich
1909   *Die Zahl 40 im Glauben, Brauch und Schrifttum der Semiten,* 7–138. Abhandlungen der Philologisch-Historischen Klasse der Königlich Sächsischen Gesellschaft der Wissenschaften. Leipzig: B.G. Teubner.
1917   Die Zahl 50 in Mythus, Kultus, Epos, und Taktik der Hellen und anderer Völker besonders der Semiten. In *Abhandlungen der Sächsischen Akademie der Wissenschaften,* no. 68. Leipzig: B.G. Teubner.

Runyan, William McKinley
1982   *Life Histories and Psychobiography: Explorations in Theory and Method.* New York: Oxford Univ. Press.

Scanlon, J.
1979   *Young Adulthood.* New York: Academy for Educational Development.

Scheper-Hughes, Nancy
1983   From Anxiety to Analysis: Rethinking Irish Sexuality and Sex Roles. *Women's Studies* 10: 147–60.

Scholes, Robert, and Robert Kellogg
1966   *The Nature of Narrative.* New York: Oxford Univ. Press.

Soddy, Kenneth, and Mary Kidson
1967   *Men in Middle Life.* London: Tavistock.

Stewart, T.D.
1962   Comments on the Reassessment of the Indian Knoll Skeletons. *American Journal of Physical Anthropology* 20:143–48.

Still, Henry
1977   *Surviving the Male Mid-Life Crisis.* New York: Crowell.

Stowe, Harriet Beecher
1852   *Uncle Tom's Cabin.* London: John Cassell.

Strand, T.A.
1958   *Tri-Ism: The Theory of the Trinity in Nature, Man and His Works.* New York: Exposition.

Targ, D.B.
1979   Toward a Reassessment of Women's Experience at Middle Age. *Family Coordinator* 28 (3): 377–82.

Tavenner, Eugene
1916   Three as a Magic Number in Latin Literature. *Trans-*

actions of the American Philological Association 47: 117–43.

Turnbull, Colin
1983　*The Human Cycle.* New York: Simon & Schuster.

Turner, Victor
1969　*The Ritual Process: Structure and Anti-Structure.* Chicago: Aldine.

Tylor, Edward B.
1958　*The Origins of Culture.* 1871. New York: Harper & Row.

Uhlenberg, Peter
1978　Changing Configurations of the Life Course. In *Transitions: The Family and the Life Course in Historical Perspective,* ed. Tamara K. Hareven, 65–98. New York: Academic Press.

Usener, H.
1903　Dreiheit. *Rheinisches Museum fur Philologie* 58:1–47, 161–208, 321–62.

Weismann, Robert
1978　*Shakespeare and the Popular Tradition in the Theater: Studies in the Social Dimension of Dramatic Form and Function.* Baltimore, Md.: Johns Hopkins Univ. Press.

Wolfenstein, Martha
1954　French Parents Take Their Children to the Park. In *Childhood in Contemporary Cultures,* ed. Margaret Mead and Martha Wolfenstein, 99–117. Chicago: Univ. of Chicago Press.

Zāda, Sheyk

1886   *The History of the Forty Vezirs; or, The Story of the Forty Morns and Eves.* Trans. E.J.W. Gibb, London: George Redway.

INDEX

148

Forty: The Age and the Symbol has been set into type on a Compugraphic digital phototypesetter in eleven point Garamond with four points of spacing between the lines. Garamond was also selected for display. The book was designed by Jim Billingsley, composed into type by Metricomp, Inc., printed offset by Thomson-Shore, Inc., and bound by John H. Dekker & Sons. The paper on which the book is printed carries acid-free characteristics designed for an effective life of at least three hundred years.

THE UNIVERSITY OF TENNESSEE PRESS : KNOXVILLE